Flash Boys:
Not So Fast

An Insider's Perspective on High-Frequency Trading

PETER KOVAC

D1413517

Directissima Press

Published by Directissima Press.

First Print Edition.

ISBN: 0692336907
ISBN-13: 978-0692336908

For those who wanted the real story

Table of Contents

PREFACE

WHAT THIS IS AND WHY

In the past few months many people have asked me to explain Michael Lewis' recent book, *Flash Boys*. The topic is quite complex, and naturally people want to know if the U.S. stock market is actually rigged, as the book claims. I wrote this piece to help them – and you – come to your own conclusion.

Flash Boys is a book about high-frequency trading that, curiously, includes no high-frequency traders. It lacks a single insider's account and, frankly, it shows. This is where I come in.

I am an industry insider, the kind of person who could have saved Lewis from making some really basic mistakes. I started programming trading strategies in 2003. After years in the trenches, I moved into management and ultimately became chief operating officer of my firm, EWT. I handled regulatory compliance, risk management, finance, trading operations, and a portion of the IT and software development teams – and I had to know every aspect of the stock market inside and out. By 2008, our company was one of the largest automated market-making firms in the U.S., trading hundreds of millions of shares of stock daily, and had expanded into many other asset classes domestically and internationally. I left it all three years ago when EWT was sold to Virtu Financial (in which, in the interest of full disclosure, I still retain a small stake).

Those eight years at EWT provided me with a front row seat to all the events described in *Flash Boys*, and much more. During that time, I shared my experience and perspective in discussions with regulators and lawmakers here and abroad, advocating for the continued improvement of the markets discussed in the book. Many of my comment letters on these topics are publicly available on the SEC website. Even though I no longer work in trading, I can still get answers from a diverse set of close sources when a truly new question arises.

As a high-frequency trader, I'd guess that Michael Lewis would dismiss my perspective out of hand. Perhaps you will do so too, but if you do you'll miss out on a very well-informed insider's view of what Lewis gets right and what he gets wrong.

If you have a copy of *Flash Boys*, treat this as a companion that you can read alongside it to help explain some of the more confusing points, and add depth and context to key areas. The chapter numbers mirror *Flash Boys*, and Lewis' examples and analyses within each chapter are addressed in the same order. If you haven't read *Flash Boys*, don't worry. I've summarized the main arguments that Lewis makes, as well as the most common counter-arguments, in the next section, entitled "The Foundations of the Debate."

With that background, we walk through the examples and arguments put forth in the book, chapter by chapter. After evaluating the *Flash Boys* case, I pull it all together in the final section, "Summing It Up." If you're more interested in the big picture than in detailed explanations of trading, just head there.

Hopefully this provides enough material to enable you to understand the more complicated aspects of Lewis' book, and, more broadly, to better understand how the U.S. stock market functions today.

The Foundations of the Debate

More than a decade ago, major stocks traded largely on one of two stock exchanges, either the New York Stock Exchange (NYSE) or the NASDAQ Stock Market. Orders on these markets were executed by a limited number of designated "market-makers" or "specialists," who had a de facto monopoly on executing orders in a particular stock. Monopolies seldom deliver the best price to their customers, however, and this arrangement was no exception. As scandal after scandal emerged documenting the abuses of this monopolistic power, it became clear that change was sorely needed.

That change arrived in the last decade, as Wall Street was upended through two important transformations to this system: computerization and competition. The result was that a couple of guys in Kansas City could connect to the exchanges in New York and, with a computer, some smarts, and a lot of *chutzpah* they could compete with the big boys on Wall Street to buy and sell shares to the public at a better price. Before Wall Street knew what hit it, folks like this – many of whom had never even been to New York – were responsible for a large portion of the trading on the exchanges.

This first "Wall Street revolt" didn't initially affect people like *Flash Boys'* protagonist Brad Katsuyama, who were "upstairs" at the banks, making the big trades that were allowed to bypass the public markets. Their clients came to them when they had a large position and didn't want to spook the markets when they dumped their shares. By mid-decade, however, the big upstairs traders started feeling the pinch, too.

Simultaneous upheaval in technology (new, faster computers; better software), regulation (completely new rules came into effect in 2007), and market structure (now there were additional exchanges instead of just NASDAQ and NYSE) made it extremely difficult for the big-bank traders to stay on top of everything. While increased competition between the now numerous market-makers had improved prices for these traders, it had also stoked clients' expectations for better prices on their trades. Perhaps more ominously, banks were now developing "trading algorithms" that aimed to replace human traders like Katsuyama altogether. And who were these high-frequency traders people were starting to talk about?

Oddly, there never has been an official definition of a "high-frequency trader," other than the obvious explanation that high-frequency trading firms must trade a lot – that is, quite frequently. Most stock market professionals would add to this definition that high-frequency trading firms employ computers to automate a substantial portion of the trading process, but that's about it for a definition.

In *Flash Boys*, Lewis never specifically tells the reader what he means by high-frequency trading. Implicitly, he adopts a circular definition in his second chapter: those who "front-run" are high-frequency traders, and high-frequency traders are the ones who "front-run." Toward the end of the book, Lewis modifies this slightly, allowing that high-frequency traders may also do other things, but these things are also mostly bad. In the end he simply admits that for him this is a term "used to obscure rather than clarify, and to put minds to early rest" – a footnote, following two-hundred plus pages of allegations of illicit and potentially criminal behavior, abdicating any responsibility to clarify whom he is accusing and whom he is not.

Interestingly, Lewis' own protagonists, Brad Katsuyama and Ronan Ryan, do seek to clarify this term by distinguishing between "good" high-frequency traders and "bad" high-frequency traders. As it turns out, the "good" high-frequency traders are ultimately responsible for a substantial amount of volume on the stock market Katsuyama ultimately launches, IEX.

In the mind of Michael Lewis, though, all high-frequency trading is destructive – and although Katsuyama's business faced a substantial array of challenges seven years ago, for Lewis the biggest threat was from high-frequency traders. Lewis argues that they targeted big bank traders like Katsuyama, inferring knowledge of his stock orders before the trades were completed and using this information to "front-run" these orders by trading before them. While they shave just fractions of a cent per share, he tells us, it adds up to vast profits for them, and a market that is rigged against everyone else. Lewis explains that nobody has stopped high-frequency trading because all the stock exchanges and regulators have a stake in the success of these high-frequency traders. In effect, he argues, the revolution of computerization was a wolf in sheep's clothing, and Katsuyama is now leading the real "Wall Street revolt."

The counter-argument is that high-frequency traders, specifically electronic market-makers, by competing with a fair set of rules, have dramatically reduced the cost of trading over the past decade, by five times or more. TD Ameritrade, the largest online retail broker, estimates that in the last ten years transaction costs have declined 80% for retail investors; Vanguard, the largest U.S. mutual fund manager, estimated that they now save $1 on every $100 of stock bought and sold. In short, everyone – retail investors, mutual funds, pension funds, whoever – has benefited significantly. In this version of the story, the only casualties of this increased efficiency are the old intermediaries who have been displaced by the computers – the Wall Street equities traders who, now, incidentally, allege this front-running conspiracy. The reason no one has found any evidence of any vast front-running conspiracy in the past ten years is that it simply isn't true. While nobody can speak for an entire industry, the vast majority of high-frequency trading firms appear to be doing no harm, and a significant portion are making the markets substantially cheaper to invest in, reducing costs and adding a little bit to everyone's investment returns.

Which is it? Is high-frequency trading one of Wall Street's greatest scams ever, as Lewis claims? Or is high-frequency trading finally bringing the computerized efficiencies of the twenty-first century to Wall Street?

INTRODUCTION

THE DANGERS OF SPEED

It's hard to understate the impact of *Flash Boys*.

The book tour headline that "the stock market is rigged" is by far the most dramatic and far-reaching thesis Michael Lewis has ever proposed. It implies that pretty much everything the American public is relying upon for retirement, be it your 401K, corporate stock plan, or your brokerage account, has been and is being robbed. In the end, Lewis alleges that the symbolic heart of global capitalism is one vast fraud, and coyly asks, "How would enterprising politicians and plaintiffs' lawyers and state attorneys general respond to this news?"

Not surprisingly, the reaction has been exactly what he looked for: multiple class-action lawsuits, Congressional hearings, and separate probes launched by the SEC, CFTC, DOJ, FINRA, NYAG, and the FBI (yes, apparently firearms are required).

No responsible journalist would make such an extraordinary claim – particularly with such far-reaching consequences – without extraordinary research. This is doubly true for a topic as complicated as electronic trading. Thus, it is utterly perplexing that in preparing *Flash Boys* Lewis apparently neglected to talk to anyone who has actually programmed a computer to trade stocks. Shouldn't a book that alleges a vast conspiracy involving more than 50% of the stock market offer at least one interview from an insider?

In contrast, Lewis went to exceptional lengths to research the remarkable telecommunications and networking technology used in electronic trading systems, conducting numerous interviews and even biking through rural Pennsylvania to trace the routes of fiber-optic cables between stock exchanges. Yet for all the stories in the book that attempt to explain why a stock exchange implemented a particular policy, there is not a single interview with anyone working at the stock exchange. For all the stories in the book that attempt to explain how a high-frequency trader does something, there is not a single interview with any high-frequency trader about trading.[1]

Why didn't Lewis actually talk to someone, anyone, who works at the stock exchanges he claims are at the center of this fraud? Why didn't he talk to a real high-frequency trader, the alleged perpetrators of the fraud, about high-frequency trading?

In his previous book, *The Big Short*, Lewis feasted upon interviews, emails, and investor reports, from inside Wall Street and everywhere else. In *Flash Boys*, the reader is served the thinnest gruel of speculation about the way high-frequency trading is done, supplied not by insiders, but by guys who are selling products marketed as warding off high-frequency traders. This is somewhat like writing a book about the dangers of commercial airlines based solely on the opinions of people who have never flown in a plane. And who happen to work for Amtrak.

The best of Lewis' immensely entertaining books have tackled complicated and controversial topics, but only after the dust had settled and the facts became clear. *Moneyball's* profile of the statistical analysis that upended baseball team management was written after the Oakland Athletics had proved the new system's

---

[1] The *only* quotation I could find from anyone involved in high-frequency trading was about the fiber-optic network between New York and Chicago. Curiously, we never hear a word from this electronic trading firm (or any

worth, reaching the playoffs in three consecutive years. *The Big Short* was published years after the protagonists banked billions betting against the US housing market, and hundreds of thousands of documents about the mortgage industry had become public through various lawsuits and regulatory probes. The genius of these books was not only in how they simplified complicated topics, but how they distilled the massive amounts of public information available to support this simplification.

Flash Boys is different. Unlike his other books, in the real world the story isn't even past the first chapter. Lewis' underdog heroes haven't conquered, banked their billions, or even been proven right. And his "villains" haven't been bankrupted, incarcerated, or proven wrong. It's not even clear who the villains are. There are no confessions from prison (or anywhere else for that matter). There are no mountains of trial evidence meticulously documenting this alleged fleecing of the public. Maybe the end is nigh for those villainized by Lewis, and we'll see them heading to prison in a few months. Or maybe not. We just don't know at this time, and, unfortunately, Lewis supplies absolutely no hard evidence to help us figure it out – instead we're stuck with a handful of theories about computerized trading, proposed by a group of outsiders who have never done computerized trading.

For a book about the dangers of speed in finance, the book itself seems rushed into print. It's therefore not surprising, although it is rather unusual, that Lewis' own "experts" have since gone out of their way to make it clear that they didn't fact-check the book, and that, in fact, they don't believe that the market is rigged.[2]

Perhaps the most surprising example of speed trumping fact checks comes in a footnote at the end of Chapter 7. Here Lewis cites academic research by Adam Clark-Joseph that he says shows how high-frequency traders (HFTs) might lose money on stock orders in

---

[2] Ronan Ryan, Chief Strategy Officer of IEX, as quoted in the article "IEX not anti-HFT, says founder," John Bakie, The TRADE, April 9, 2014.

order to make more money elsewhere. Perhaps Lewis didn't have time to actually read the research paper to which he is referring, which states on its third page:

> "One possibility is that HFTs merely react to public information faster than everyone else...a second possibility is that the HFTs simply front-run coming demand when they can predict future orders. **However, I find neither of these hypotheses to be consistent with the data.**"[3]

In other words, this research, cited by Lewis himself near the conclusion of his book, contradicts everything he has said about front-running in the prior two hundred pages.

In fairness, neither contradicting academic research nor the lack of access to insiders or evidence disprove Lewis' hypothesis. He still could be right. But these factors do make it more difficult for a critical reader to believe that this is a complete picture of the markets. Regardless, it's worth considering his arguments carefully. For if he is wrong, there's quite a mess to clean up. And if he is right, we have even more serious problems in our country.

Let's take a look at what Michael Lewis has dug up this time.

---

[3] See "Exploratory Trading," Adam Clark-Joseph, Job Market Paper. January 13, 2013 (emphasis added).

CHAPTER 1:

SPREAD NETWORKS AND THE VALUE OF SPEED

The first chapter is Michael Lewis at his best: how many other authors can make a story about laying fiber-optic cable through rural Pennsylvania a page-turner?

Why Does Speed Matter (and When Does It Not)?

It's a classic story of somebody who saw an opportunity, and made a huge bet that paid off. From everyone I've talked to in the industry, and from my own experience, the story Lewis tells of Spread Networks is quite accurate, down to the pricing of $176k per month. Lots of people paid lots of money so that their stock market data and orders would travel between Chicago and New York in 13 milliseconds instead of 16 milliseconds.

Why? Does speed really matter?

Yes.

Imagine that you plan to sell your house. You'd like to set a fair price that reflects the market's current value. If your real estate broker provides you with a list of sales in your zip code from 2002, it's basically worthless. A list of sales from last year provides some value. A list of sales from the past few months is actually quite helpful, and weekly updates wouldn't hurt. The more up-to-date your information is, the more accurately and precisely you can set your price.

The stock markets operate in a similar manner. Faster dissemination of market pricing information enables market participants to adjust their quotes quickly. This allows the market to make prices that are more precise. If you look back at the last decade, you'll see that as the delays in the market decrease, so too does the cost of trading decrease. Ten years ago, when markets were slower, the difference between the market price to buy and sell shares of Microsoft might have been six cents a share. This six-cent difference per share is what you effectively paid (in addition to your brokerage commissions) to invest in Microsoft and later realize your gains. In other words, about 0.20% of your investment was lost as "economic friction." In today's superfast markets, the difference between the market price to buy and sell Microsoft has dropped to about a penny, or 0.03%. The increased speed and automation facilitated more precise prices, and we investors have benefited tremendously. Every penny of that reduction in "economic friction" is a cash bonus that goes straight to your pocketbook.

But if the difference between the price to buy and the price to sell is now just a penny, how much more benefit is there to be had? Why are market participants still looking to go faster if they can't make their prices any more precise?

The answer is: competition. If they don't get faster and their competitors do, they lose. Who are these competitors? Pretty much everyone who does this for a living: hedge fund traders, big bank traders, high-frequency traders, day traders, you name it. Who isn't a competitor? You, actually.

Individual investors are, happily, insulated from the arms race to go faster and faster. It doesn't matter whether you or I are faster or slower than the professional traders, because we are doing different things. The professionals race each other to react to new market-wide information. New information is broadcast – Microsoft beat earning expectations last quarter – and the pros race to be the first to adjust their resting prices and trade Microsoft shares.

For individual investors there is no race at all. You invest because you decided that you wanted to. Nobody else in the market knows why or when you made this choice, so nobody could race you if they wanted to. When you place your market order to buy shares in Apple, it executes the instant it hits the market. The pros never even see your order coming. They only see the trade created by your order, after it has already executed and become a part of history. Speed doesn't matter for individual investors, since there is no race to be run.

Still, speed matters for the pros. It matters relative to their competitors. And so, as Lewis puts it, the professionals had no choice but to pay Spread Networks millions to "enjoy the right to continue doing what they were already doing."[4]

Spread Networks

The economics of electronic trading prior to Spread Networks' launch were simple. All you needed to trade electronically was a computer, a network connection, and lots of smarts. For a few brief years, the barriers to entry in the industry were quite low (well, except for the last requirement). At every other time in history, it has been extremely difficult to break into the stock market. Aside from incredibly high trading costs, oligopolistic systems of bequeathed trading privileges made it almost impossible for new participants. If

---

[4] On an annualized basis, the five-year Spread Networks contract plus equipment would total approximately $2.8 million per year. It's not clear why, but before the chapter ends this has become "tens of millions of dollars in entry fees." Chapter 3 runs with the new inflated figure, citing "the tens of millions being spent by high-frequency traders for tiny increments of speed."

you were one of the lucky few who owned a "seat" at the NYSE, you could trade directly; if not, you had to pay some broker who did own a seat to trade for you. The advent of electronic trading a decade ago eliminated these barriers to entry and created a huge democratization of trading that undermined much of Wall Street's traditional hold on the markets. Not coincidentally, as competition flourished, trading costs plummeted.

The emergence of Spread – "the biggest what-the-fuck moment the industry had had in some time," per Lewis – changed these economics dramatically. One reason that trading firms were circumspect about the profits that they made is that, quite simply, they were worried that someone in their supply chain (e.g. Verizon) might decide to ratchet up their prices simply because they could. This is exactly what Spread did.

It's not unlike a landlord waking up one moment and realizing that the McDonald's in his mall is more profitable than any other fast food joint, and then doubling its rent, just because he can.[5] Free market economists would call this the natural extension of monopoly pricing (Spread had no competitors). Business school professors would call the move brilliant. Others might call it cutthroat. Personally, I think it was all three.

Lewis tries to temper the cutthroat angle by explaining that this new rent was being extracted from "the people on Wall Street then making perhaps more money than people had ever made on Wall Street." This is, in fact, the first time the reader is introduced to high-frequency traders, and Lewis wants to quash any sympathy one might have for the guys forced to pay Spread for the right to continue doing what they were already doing. Who could shed a tear for someone who makes even more money than a hedge fund manager?

---

[5] Coincidentally, the average McDonald's has expenses of about $175k per month, about the same amount – $176k per month – that that Spread's five-year $10.6 million contract cost.

But were these guys really making more money than people had ever made on Wall Street? Reading ahead, one doubts that anyone, Lewis included, believes this. Although he doesn't attempt to substantiate this claim here, in Chapter 5, Lewis tosses out a vague number: "financial intermediaries" on Wall Street made between $10 and $22 billion per year in total profits. How does this stack up to the rest of Wall Street? At this point in his story – early 2010 – Goldman Sachs had just paid $16.2 billion to its employees in compensation, out of revenues of $45.2 billion for the previous year. In other words, Goldman alone paid more in *bonuses and salaries* than the *total profits* of all high-frequency trading firms (plus whoever else he lumped in as "financial intermediaries.")

So, perhaps, they weren't making "more money than people had ever made on Wall Street." Admittedly, they weren't paupers. But they also weren't even in the same league as hedge funds and banks.

CHAPTER 2:

THE EDUCATION OF BRAD KATSUYAMA

The most important thing to know about the background of *Flash Boys'* hero, Brad Katsuyama, is what exactly he did for a living. Lewis describes his job well, "to sit between investors who wanted to buy and sell big amounts of stock and the public market, where the volumes were smaller." Katsuyama was the quintessential financial intermediary. Royal Bank of Canada (RBC) paid him $2 million a year for taking these large orders for stocks and, as Lewis puts it, working artfully over hours to unload the shares onto the public markets.

The reason RBC's clients paid so much for this service – in the first example in the book, the client paid RBC over a quarter of a million dollars for a single trade – was that the banks had convinced large investors that the markets were extremely complex, and that large orders required the special expertise and artistry that traders like Katsuyama brought to the table. A large order would impact the price of a stock and move the markets, and clients should leave managing those risks to the banks. The banks performed a valuable, if expensive, service as an intermediary. However, at some point the relative expertise that they sold to big investors was no longer as expert as it used to be.

The Market Behaves Unexpectedly: The Case of Solectron

Our first foray into trading begins with Katsuyama realizing that, "at almost exactly the moment" that he got a new trading system, "the U.S. stock market began to behave oddly." After pages and pages of describing how ignorant, crude and inept the creators of this new system were, Lewis comes to the punch line: "Until [Katsuyama] was forced to use some of Carlin's technology, he trusted his trading screens...Now the market as it appeared on his screens was an illusion."

Yet, apparently, none of this odd behavior was related to the newly deployed trading technology. Rather, it seems that Katsuyama began to suspect that the oddities on his trading screens were instead signs of new, unseen predators operating in the markets.

These suspicions were born when he was given the job of selling five million shares of Solectron, a company about to be acquired:

> "[The market for Solectron] was 3.70-3.75, which is to say you could sell Solectron for $3.70 a share or buy it for $3.75. The problem was that, at those prices, only a million shares were bid for and offered. The big investor who wished to sell 5 million shares of Solectron called Brad because he wanted Brad to take the risk on the other 4 million shares. And so Brad bought the shares at $3.65, slightly below the price quoted in the public markets. But when he turned to the public markets – the markets on his trading screens – the share price instantly moved. Almost as if the market had read his mind. Instead of selling a million shares at $3.70, as he'd assumed he could do, he sold a few hundred thousand and triggered a minicollapse in the price of Solectron. It was as if someone knew what he was trying to do and was reacting to his desire to sell before he had fully expressed it. By the time he was done selling all 5 million shares, at prices far below $3.70, he had lost a small fortune."

Let's assume that "when he turned to the public markets the share price instantly moved" is more of a turn of phrase than an accurate chronological retelling, for Lewis admits that Katsuyama did sell a few hundred thousand shares – probably over a million dollars' worth of stock – at the stated price. Instead of mind-reading, then, it's clear that Katsuyama's trade itself triggered a minicollapse in the price of the stock.

Lewis tells us that this made no sense to Katsuyama, since he thought that Solectron was going to be acquired at a known price and he had therefore assumed that the current market price shouldn't move. Yet Katsuyama's client was willing to sell his shares to Katsuyama for five cents below the current market price – a built in loss of $250,000. If the price should be absolutely stable, why would that client have paid a quarter of a million dollars to Katsuyama to "artfully work" this order?

The answer is that, of course, the price is not actually stable. While the price of the acquisition may be known, whether or not the acquisition will actually happen is not known at all. In fact, there is an entire slice of the hedge fund world called "merger arbitrage" that places bets on whether or not such mergers or acquisitions happen. If the hedge fund thinks that the acquisition will definitely happen, it will buy any shares available if they are below the acquisition price. Conversely, if it thinks that the acquisition will not happen, it is willing to sell shares – and even sell them for less than the acquisition price, since the share price often collapses catastrophically when an acquisition attempt fails. The fact that merger arbitrage is a large and profitable business indicates that the prices of merger targets are far from stable.

That is why the stock of an acquisition target trades in a narrow range, but is incredibly fragile: if there is a big sale, some merger arbitrage hedge fund immediately worries that another hedge fund has learned that the acquisition has fallen apart, and the stock is about to collapse.

Imagine that you have a $50 gift card to Wild Oats, a grocery store about to be acquired by Whole Foods. The local store says that Whole Foods will probably honor the gift card after the acquisition. If I offered to sell you my Wild Oats gift card for $49 – I know I'm losing money but I don't feel like standing in line and exchanging the card next month – you'd probably buy it. But if I offered to sell you 100 gift cards at $40 a piece – hey, you'll make $1000, sound like a deal? – you might start to wonder why I was so eager to sell at an obvious loss. Just like a used car salesman hawking a lemon as a great deal, you might wonder what the seller knows that you don't. In other words, you'd be pretty suspicious that the gift cards could be worthless, and definitely not worth $40.

If he didn't want to spook the market, Katsuyama could have offered his shares for sale at the current offer price of $3.75 and waited for someone to buy, or offered his shares even cheaper at $3.74 in order to be the first in line to sell his shares. If he believed that the shares would trade in a narrow price band, this would make sense. (He would also make $0.09 or $0.10 cents a share in total profit, almost half a million dollars.) Instead, he sells hundreds of thousands of shares at the bid price of $3.70. Maybe in a non-acquisition target stock the price would dip, then rebound, and he could get away with this. But with an acquisition target, he just shouted at the market that somebody wants out of Solectron so badly that he'll sell well below the acquisition price. Predictably, the market panics, thinking somebody knows some reason that Solectron won't be acquired and the deal won't go through. The stock collapses. While regrettable, Katsuyama's loss is simply the result of market pricing. It seems like a stretch to blame some invisible predator for his troubles.[6]

---

[6] Later in this chapter Lewis tells us that front-running high-frequency traders buy and sell nearly instantaneously – at most, within a few seconds. In contrast, Katsuyama would "work artfully over the next few hours to unload the other 2 million shares." In Lewis' construction, if Katsuyama took the time to sneeze, these alleged front-runners would be long gone. Yet

Looking at the numbers, it's actually quite a stretch. Katsuyama's client sold the shares to him at a price $0.05 below the current bid, and $0.075 below the midpoint of the bid and offer. This is a built-in profit of $250,000 to $375,000 for Katsuyama. Yet he winds up losing "a small fortune" – at least his built-in profit of $250,000, we can assume, and maybe more. Lewis claims later in this chapter that high-frequency front-running costs Katsuyama an average of $0.0029 per share. If one assumes that (a) there really is a high-frequency front-running conspiracy, and (b) Lewis' estimates are correct, this conspiracy theory would only explain $14,500 of Katsuyama's loss of $250,000. Put another way, the loss due to Katsuyama triggering the collapse is at least 16 times greater than any loss Lewis would ascribe to high-frequency front-running. Katsuyama would have to be exquisitely attuned to the market and his own trading to distinguish between the 94% of the error due to him and the 6% he claims is due to somebody else. It's like a batter who has struck out seventeen times in a row claiming that the eleventh strike-out wasn't his fault because on that one the pitcher secretly threw a spitball – it's possible, but a little hard to believe. It's even harder to believe when Katsuyama simultaneously complains that his trading system can't even provide him with accurate data.

One can't rule out the possibility that some computerized predator outsmarted Katsuyama as he dumped a million shares on the market. But it seems more likely that Economics 101 was to blame. In the law of supply and demand, if you increase the supply, the price falls.

---

apparently he continued to lose money as he worked artfully over the next few hours?

The Market Behaves Unexpectedly (again): The Case of AMGN

> *"'Watch closely. I'm about to buy one hundred thousand shares of AMGN. I am willing to pay forty-eight dollars a share. There are currently one hundred thousand shares of AMGN being offered at forty-eight dollars a share – ten thousand on BATS, thiry-five thousand on the New York Stock Exchange, thirty thousand on Nasdaq, and twenty-five thousand on Direct Edge.' You could see it all on the screens."[7]*

As Katsuyama investigates the market's reaction to his trades, he tries an experiment with the tech stock AMGN. After waiting for a quiet period in the market, he tries to buy 100,000 shares in one fell swoop (about $4.8 million of stock). The stock pops higher. Katsuyama ominously explains to his team, "I'm the event. I *am* the news."

Brad's statement that he is the news isn't exactly revelatory. He tried to dump a huge number of shares on the market, and the market, hewing to the basic economic laws of supply and demand, reacted. Traders call this phenomenon "price impact," and it's something that Katsuyama's colleagues at RBC were well aware of. When Lewis later describes the work of his colleague Rob Park to create a trading algorithm, he explains, "No smart trader seeking to buy 100,000 shares would tip his desire for a mere 100 shares." Or, describing the purpose of a dark pool, Lewis writes, "If, say Fidelity

---

[7] In the initial Kindle version of *Flash Boys*, released simultaneously with the print version, Lewis says the stock is not AMGN, but rather AMD. AMD occasionally has 100,000 shares offered but has never traded near $48. AMGN traded at $48 at the end of 2007, but typically has only a few hundred shares on offer. A later Kindle version changes the price to $4 in one place but retains $48 in another place. Since none of the print or electronic versions of the anecdote align with reality (or each other), I arbitrarily used the print version in this example. It's a little disconcerting, to say the least, that the basic facts of one of the very few actual trading anecdotes continue to change (and various editions of *Flash Boys* fail to acknowledge this).

wanted to sell a million shares of Microsoft, Corp....[o]n the public exchanges, everyone would notice a big seller had entered the market, and the market price of Microsoft would plunge."

Katsuyama's job was to minimize price impact. The fact that Katsuyama had this skill and others did not is the reason his client paid Katsuyama $0.05 per share of Solectron to sell millions of shares. The client assumed that if he sold the shares himself, he would lose more than five cents per share due to price impact. On the other hand, Katsuyama would, as Lewis writes, "work artfully over the next few hours" to minimize that price impact. The strange thing is that, at some point, Katsuyama no longer portrays himself as the master of managing price impact, but as the victim of price impact. It was as if, having found someone to blame, he simply gave up trying, and inartfully dumped millions of dollars of stock onto the market in a single instantaneous blast.

While it may seem sinister to Katsuyama at first that the market doesn't behave the way he wants it to, it's also economically predictable. Again, supply and demand affect price. The market doesn't "pop" due to a conspiracy of predators, it "pops" because Katsuyama suddenly changed the supply of shares. In other words, the market behaves exactly as you'd expect a market to behave.

Maker-taker: What is it and Why?

The first time I ever heard anyone say that the maker-taker pricing model was "incredibly complicated" and "understood by almost no one" was in *Flash Boys*. Airline fees, perhaps, are incredibly complicated, but exchange fees are not.

What is "maker-taker"? The idea behind maker-taker pricing is to incentivize the "market-makers" who stick their necks out and promise to pay a certain price for a stock. The maker places a "limit" order in the market, which is a promise to buy or sell at a particular price. This order rests in the market until somebody agrees to "take" that price, the order is canceled, or the market closes for the day. The problem is that placing such a resting order is a risky proposition, and few are willing to take that risk.

Everyone has heard the rule that in negotiations one should never be the first one to give a number. The person who goes first always risks lowballing themselves, or pricing themselves out of the market completely. There's a decent risk that, whatever number they pick, it won't be the optimal one. Worse still, this isn't a negotiation between two parties. When the maker sticks their neck out, they give every other person in the market the option to either take the number they pick, or to leave it. It's them against the world.

Imagine that a market-maker has submitted a resting bid to buy Microsoft shares at $39.40. If negative news comes out about Microsoft, be it a lawsuit, missed sales numbers, or whatever, the value of Microsoft plummets and the race is on: the maker against the entire market. If a single taker comes and picks off this (now) overvalued price, the maker stands to lose quite a bit. If the maker beats everyone else to the punch, their only reward is the chance to stick their neck out again and guess at a new price.

The question, then, is how to encourage the maker to take on this risk. The "maker-taker" model of rebates for these makers is one answer to that question: pay the maker a nominal amount of money as compensation for taking that risk.

Why do exchanges pay market-makers? Historically, almost every exchange has compensated market-makers in some way, because if nobody puts resting orders into the market, then there is no market. Usually the compensation was in the form of a monopoly, where a single market-maker was designated and had preferential priority on all trades, as well as preferential pricing. When the markets were opened to competition over ten years ago, these privileges disappeared. The idea of rebating market-makers a small amount on each trade was created as a more fair and equitable way to incent multiple market-makers to make markets on an exchange.

As an exchange gains liquidity – that is, more resting bids and offers for the takers to trade against – more participants come to the market, and volume starts to increase in a self-perpetuating cycle. At some point, the exchange may determine that it doesn't need to rebate as much to market-makers, and it may adjust its fees accordingly.

The exchange may even decide to "invert" the fees, paying a rebate to takers and charging makers. This obviously incentivizes takers to access the prices on that exchange instead of other exchanges (where they would have to pay to trade), and results in more trades on that exchange. The theory in this case is that the makers won't abandon that now-expensive exchange, because the increased trading volume may offset the losses they incur from the increased fees. Sometimes this works, sometimes it doesn't.

How much does a maker get paid? The maker is typically rebated two tenths of a penny per share for their trouble, if a trade actually occurs. Nothing is paid if no trade occurs. Of course, if the stock drops by just a penny, this profit is wiped out, five times over. Not exactly the "kickback" arrangement that Lewis portrays. (*Flash Boys* says that, "the exchanges charged takers a few pennies a share, paid makers somewhat less, and pocketed the difference." This is wrong. In reality, the highest fees for takers are typically three tenths of a penny per share, about ten times less than what Lewis says. The fees are posted on every exchange's website.)

The remarkable thing is that two tenths of a cent per share is enough of an incentive for some people to make markets for a living. Obviously they must have very low costs and be able to tolerate absurdly low profit margins. How low? Most industry analysts peg market-maker gross profit margins at less than a tenth of a cent per share, or a gross profit margin of 0.01%.[8] For comparison, Amazon's gross profit margins are 28.8% and Wal-Mart has the lowest gross profit margins in retail at 24.87% – more than a thousand times higher.[9]

These razor thin margins can work, however, as long as a market-maker trades often enough. To do so, they also have to be extremely good at providing the absolute best price in the market at all times – a trade can only occur when they offer the best price (and are first in line at that price), and they can only make money when they trade. Imagine if the same law of best execution applied to retail, and Wal-Mart could only sell a product if they matched or beat the best price displayed anywhere in the country. Obviously the consumer would benefit through even lower prices, and the same principle applies to the markets – the bruising battles among market-makers to set the best price have many losers, but the investor on the other side of the trade always wins by getting the best possible price.

Who are the market-makers? Market-makers are, by default, high-frequency traders. As one would expect from a firm that is always willing to buy and sell at the best price, they trade frequently. Also as one would expect, the only way to handle a large volume of trades is through automation. Thus, under the broad definition of high-frequency trading as trading frequently using computers, market-making is high-frequency trading.

However, many high-frequency traders are not market-makers. Many trading strategies – in fact, almost all hedge fund trading

---

[8] See "How the Robots Lost: High-Frequency Trading's Rise and Fall," Mathew Phillips, Businessweek, June 6, 2013.

[9] See "Amazon Again Reports Thin Profits," Alistair Barr, The Wall Street Journal, April 24, 2014. See also "Walmart and Target Have the Worst Gross Profit Margin Among Peers," Celan Bryant, The Motley Fool, January 21, 2014.

strategies – are not market-making strategies, but are designed to profit in some other way entirely. For example, in Chapter 7 Lewis describes a common relative value strategy, trading the statistical relationship between Chevron and Exxon. There are in fact a myriad of such trading strategies out there, and in the end electronic market-making is but one slice of the high-frequency trading world.

Why do exchanges have different fees? Exchanges compete with each other. The product they offer – executing trades – is a commodity. One of the few places commodity vendors can differentiate themselves from their competitors is through price. Thus, it's not surprising that the exchanges would charge different fees. The only surprising angle is that the head of equities trading at a major bank had to Google this to learn it.

The Real Questions. Although *Flash Boys* uses maker-taker pricing mainly as a mildly amusing foil for the complexity of the markets, there are a number of real policy questions, posed by the SEC and many others, about whether or it is a good idea:

1) Fragmentation. By providing another dimension for competition, does this model encourage too many new exchanges? Or does fragmentation occur for other reasons? Would restricting price competition among exchanges impact fragmentation?

2) Winners and losers. Generally, guys like Katsuyama who take liquidity pay the most under the maker-taker model. If, from a policy perspective, we want to help them at the expense of the market-makers, it makes sense to ban maker-taker. On the other hand, if we don't want policy to favor one class of traders over another, pricing should be determined by market forces.

3) <u>Needless complexity.</u> Does the maker-taker model create needless economic complexity in our markets? Or can traders easily account for this in their trading models?

4) <u>Best execution.</u> Does maker-taker pricing create unhealthy incentives for the "best price" fiduciary responsibility of brokers with respect to their client orders? The fees and rebates flow to the broker, while the price of the shares is passed along to the client.

It's beyond the scope of this piece to delve into these issues, but hopefully the regulators will be able to resume addressing these issues after the fracas over *Flash Boys* quiets down. There is quite a bit to ponder in this area.

The Market Isn't An Illusion – But It Doesn't Wait For You, Either

"What people saw when they looked at the U.S. stock market – the numbers on the screens of the professional traders, the ticker tape running across the bottom of the CNBC screen – was an illusion. 'That's when I realized the markets are rigged.'"

In the 1930s, newspaper magnate William Randolph Hearst paid to have newspapers flown in every morning to his remote beachside estate, so that he would always have the latest news. Today, with an iPhone in hand, we can see the news as soon as it hits the wire service (or Twitter as the case may be), and scoff at Hearst's view of the news, which was of course "yesterday's news." However, the story read on the iPhone is also not current, for it took time to write and post to the Internet. An Instagram photo takes time to send, and even "live" video takes time to upload, rendering our buffered viewing seconds out of date. We can get tantalizingly close to a perfect view of the world as it exists at this instant, but, in the end, we will never be able to have a perfect instantaneous view. It takes time for information to get to us, and while that information is travelling the rest of the world doesn't wait.

The markets are no different. Curiously, while individual investors understand this, some professionals do not. I open the newspaper and see the prices from yesterday, and know that if I call my broker to trade today I'll probably get a slightly different price. Even if I go online to Google Finance to see today's prices, the website makes it clear that the prices displayed are at least fifteen minutes old. I know that if I placed an order to buy at the "market" price, I might get the price displayed, I might get a slightly better price, or I might get a slightly worse price.

Intuitively, this isn't surprising. It's common sense that prices can change when you (or your data) are *en route*. The gas station may have said $4.12 per gallon when my wife drove by it yesterday, but when I drive over and fill up today, it may be $4.11 or $4.13. The world doesn't wait for me while I receive information and process it, and I don't expect it to.

Oddly, Katsuyama and his trader colleagues at RBC apparently did expect the world to wait while they received and processed their stock market information. They knew that, for individual investors, stock prices might change between the time that you or I saw the price and when we placed our orders. But they expected that they were different. They expected that their personal Bloomberg terminals and their bank's custom computerized trading platform not only delivered stock prices to them faster than individual investors, but that it somehow guaranteed that the prices on their screens would remain there until they decided to act on it. In effect, they believed that they were entitled to whatever price they had seen at the gas station yesterday, even if the rest of us weren't. When they realized that, just like everyone else, the prices they were seeing were yesterday's news, they declared the market was rigged.

Perhaps the precision of prices in today's markets also confused them. Fifteen years ago, stocks were *not allowed* to be priced in pennies – all prices had to be rounded to the nearest fraction of a dollar. Today, stocks can be priced in penny increments. While more precise prices mean you get a better deal, it also means the prices change more often. Imagine your grocery store used to only trade in dollars: milk was $5 a gallon, eggs were $3 a dozen. These prices almost never changed. Then the grocery store starts using pennies: milk is now $4.69 a gallon, eggs are $2.89 a dozen. Next week the prices might be a nickel higher or lower. The new system means (a) prices change more frequently than previously, but (b) the more precise prices allow you to get a better deal. So it goes in the stock market. Now that prices are allowed to be more precise, they change more frequently – but the prices are more accurate and investors get a better deal.

Until reading this book, I hadn't seen any professionals – whether high-frequency traders or not – who expected that the market would wait for them. Every high-frequency trader I have spoken to "misses" on a lot of their orders – that is, they see a price on a certain market, but the price changes before their order reaches that market. The simple fact is that every single price you see, whether or not you have a super-computer, is old news. The price represents a single moment in time, and you received that price data at a later moment in time. The idea of "perfect market data" is delusional.[10]

Despite this, Lewis writes later in Chapter 3 that, "The haves enjoyed a perfect view of the market; the have-nots never saw the market at all." If nothing else, this underscores the fact that Lewis did not talk to anyone who really does electronic trading – they know all too well that there is no such thing as "a perfect view of the market." Geography, for one, makes it impossible. Imagine that you and I meet

---

[10] James Angel of Georgetown University's McDonough School of Business presents a good overview of the topic in a recent paper, summing up the *impossibility* of perfect market data thusly: "Observers in different locations may simultaneously observe different 'best' prices." See "When Finance Meets Physics: The Impact of the Speed of Light on Financial Markets and their Regulation," James Angel, *The Financial Review*, May 2014.

in New York and synchronize our watches. I then travel to New Jersey, while you stay in New York. Now I tell my computer to send you the current time on my watch, and you compare it to your watch. Due to the time to transmit the message, you will find that my "current time" is a few milliseconds slower than yours. Now you tell your computers to send me the current time on your watch. I find that your "current time" is a few milliseconds slower than mine, for the same reason! It doesn't matter how fast or fancy our watches or computers are, neither of us can ever have a perfect picture of what is going on *this instant* in two different places.

Even in a single place it's not possible to have perfect data. For example, imagine there are 5,000 shares offered for sale on the NYSE. Now, two separate orders to purchase shares arrive, the first order to purchase 2,000 shares and the second order to purchase the remaining 3,000 shares. After the first order is processed, the NYSE broadcasts the trade and the fact that there are now only 3,000 shares left. When I receive that message, I decide to want to purchase some shares too. I generate my purchase order, not knowing that the other order – already in line at the NYSE – is guaranteed to buy the rest of the shares. By the time I've sent my order in, the shares are already gone. In truth, I never had a chance. The other order was already *en route*. It doesn't matter whether I am sitting at the NYSE and it doesn't matter if I have the world's fastest computer. It is impossible to have perfect data, no matter what technology you have.

This makes it all the more remarkable that, by the end of the book, Katsuyama suddenly comes to believe that he has acquired a perfect view of the market. When he starts his dark pool IEX, his analysts pore over market data and describe the strategies they think high-frequency traders must do, based on the data that they see.[11] We'll evaluate the plausibility of such strategies in Chapter 7,

---

[11] Even at that point in the book, Lewis and Katsuyama still haven't found any high-frequency traders to actually explain what they do, so they have to guess.

but for now recognize that any such analysis assumes absolutely perfect data. Which simply isn't possible.

But if there is no such thing as perfect data, is it even possible to trade in the markets? Of course.

Test it yourself. Go to your broker and place a "market order." Your trade executes immediately at the current market price. Place a "limit order" for a particular price. If your price matches any other price in the market, you will trade at the price you asked for, or even a better price. The fact is that every visible order on a stock exchange can and will trade if it matches the price of another order on that exchange.

Individual investors understand this. They aren't the ones complaining about not getting the prices they want – the old guard equity trading shops are. If you listen carefully, the complaint isn't even that they can't trade at the market price, but rather that they can't trade *an entire large block of shares without paying a single penny more to do so.* The stock exchanges not only track orders to purchase and sell at the best market price, but also orders to purchase and sell for all other prices. Almost always, there are even more shares available if you want to pay an extra penny to get them. As Gregg Berman, Associate Director of the SEC's Office of Analytics and Research, puts it:

> "If you need to trade more shares than are posted at the prevailing spread, you can if you are willing to pay a penny or two more. But apparently, this is far from the norm.

> Frankly, I find these results rather unsettling. They suggest that modern market structure has evolved to the point where liquidity takers, including buy-side participants, focus their trading efforts on nothing more than what's available at the NBBO."[12]

---

[12] See "What Drives the Complexity and Speed of our Markets?" Gregg Berman, North American Trading Architecture Summit, April 15, 2014. See: http://www.sec.gov/News/Speech/Detail/Speech/1370541505819.

In other words, buy-side traders like Katsuyama sometimes want more shares than the market has to offer at the best price. The extra shares they want are available if they pay a penny more to access the "depth" of the order book. They simply choose not to do so, instead gambling that they can outrun their own price impact and capture that extra penny for themselves. If they win, they can pocket a bigger bonus; and if they lose, they can always blame phantom "front-runners."[13]

Flash Orders

Flash orders were perhaps the dumbest idea yet in the electronic markets. Lewis is absolutely right to heap scorn on the idea. So, what were "flash orders"?

Before answering that, let us make a very important distinction. An order is a desire to buy or sell shares at a particular price. A trade is a completed transaction at a particular price. In general, an order is not visible to anyone else in the market unless the customer chooses it to be. In contrast, a trade is visible to the whole market. Even if part of the order results in a trade, information about the remainder of the order is still not visible to the market unless the customer chooses it to be.[14]

---

[13] Berman notes that by using an "ISO" order the trader would be "*guaranteed* to be filled at depth since quotes cannot be canceled once such an order is received by the exchange." This order type, available everywhere since 2007, avoids the "disappearing shares" problem of which Katsuyama complains. *Ibid*, emphasis added.

[14] If a trader uses a displayed limit order, then, by their own choice, information on price and quantity are shared with the market. The majority of the examples in *Flash Boys* involve market orders, where neither price nor quantity is shared publicly. Only when a trade occurs do the price and quantity of the trade (but not the original order) become public.

For example, if a market order to purchase 10,000 shares is submitted and trades against a resting offer to sell 2,000 shares, the market sees only a trade of 2,000 shares at the offering price. No information about the market order is disseminated – not the price desired, not the quantity of shares desired, not even the existence of the order is shared with anyone else. The only person who knows about the remaining 8,000 shares that did not execute is the person who sent that order.

This distinction is important, since sometimes in *Flash Boys* these lines are blurred – when a private market order results in a public trade, and it's implied that the general public now knows the details of that private market order. This is simply not true.

There was one notable exception in the past. Until early 2011, the exchange Direct Edge had a program where, if an order were not immediately executed, brokers could choose to "flash" the order for a brief period of time before sending it to another exchange for execution. Direct Edge argued that this "flash" might attract a counterparty to the trade, making it more likely that the customer's order would execute, and sometimes even resulting in a better price. However, many participants saw this disclosure of the order information as a breach of the unwritten rule that market order information is private. Even if it might provide benefits in some cases, flash orders that revealed private order intentions would for the first time make it possible to trade ahead of an electronic order. This possibility could – and did – give the industry a black eye.

Interestingly, the largest critic of "flash orders" was not Katsuyama or RBC (in fact, I have seen no evidence of any criticism on their part). The largest critic was the largest high-frequency trader, Getco. If this was a conspiracy, it was not a very cohesive one.

Thor Works, Proving That Thor Works

Until this point in the book, Lewis has given us two or three examples of the markets behaving in ways that he can't / doesn't explain. While he mentions price impact in many other places later in the book, at this point these supposedly sinister examples are attributed solely to the mysterious new high-frequency traders, leading us to the point in the story where he finally proposes his theory:

> "Someone out there was using the fact that stock market orders arrived at different times at different exchanges to front-run orders from one market to another."

This is an extremely serious allegation. Not only would this be highly unethical, it is clearly illegal.[15] Let us examine what exactly led Lewis to this conclusion.

This claim is apparently based upon Katsuyama and fellow RBC employee Rob Park's observation of how the market reacts to two different types of trades. When trading by hand, they execute part of their desired trade, but the market reacts quickly and they cannot get the remainder of their trade executed at the price that they want. When they execute with Thor, which trades simultaneously everywhere, they get the price they want on all markets.

That's it. That is the basis of their claim of front-running. There is no analysis of other contemporaneous market trades, or even other market prices around the time of Katsuyama's two trades – not one bit of data that demonstrates how *others* reacted to the trades. The foundation of the theory that more than half of the stock market is front-running the remainder of the stock market is based solely on

---

[15] In an interview with 60 Minutes, Lewis has said that this would be "perfectly legal." This is wrong. The scheme described by Lewis requires manipulating the market to drive up the price of a stock, which is illegal under Section 9(a)(2) of the Securities and Exchange Act of 1934.

FLASH BOYS: NOT SO FAST

the fact that one thing Katsuyama did worked, and another thing didn't.

Nevertheless, it is interesting: why does Thor work? If we return to the gas station metaphor, imagine this: pre-Thor, Katsuyama would go to each gas station in town, one at a time, and buy *all* the gasoline they had. Pretty soon, people hear there is a run on gasoline and the price starts to rise before Katsuyama can get to the last stations. With Thor, he sends his traders to each gas station, watches synchronized to arrive at the exact same time. The stations get cleaned out simultaneously, before anyone knows that there is a run on gasoline. The price still jumps up afterward, but Katsuyama got the low price he wanted on every drop of gasoline – the price impact of his trade is now 100% somebody else's problem.

This is exactly how it plays out in the markets. Market-makers earn their living by being willing to buy and sell a stock all day long. Their profit is the difference ("spread") between the bid and the offer price. For example, a market-maker might be willing to buy XYZ for $40.14 and sell it for $40.15. If someone buys the shares from them, the market remains stable, and somebody else later sells those shares back, they make a penny per share. It's not much, but when done often enough it can be profitable. However, they can also lose a lot of money if the market moves in the time between when they sold the shares and when they bought them back. How do market-makers find out that the market is moving? Usually the hard way – somebody dumps a lot of stock on them as the market drops, and they're stuck with a losing position, scrambling to minimize their losses.

Now imagine you are a market-maker. How would you minimize this risk? If you see somebody dump 10,000 shares on the market-maker next to you, and then another 15,000 shares on the market-maker next to him, will you still be willing to buy XYZ at the same price? Or would you adjust your price, so you aren't left holding the bag after the market drops?

This is exactly what the SEC staffer in Chapter 4 means when he explains to Brad that, "You're not letting them get out of the way."[16] Effectively, Thor is blitzing the market-makers, pouncing before they have a chance to adjust their market price to account for the surge in supply or demand. As Katsuyama said, "I am the event" – but only Thor knows about that event. The market-makers never see it coming. Thor has a distinct information advantage on the market-makers, and they get hammered.

This doesn't mean Thor was unethical, illegal, or even unsavory. It was a clever tool that outsmarted the market-makers.[17] Eventually, Thor stopped working, probably due to market-makers reducing their exposure by adjusting their prices more quickly when a large trade happened. Thus, in a full circle of irony, Thor probably encouraged the small-scale volatility and skittishness of the markets that it was designed to avoid.

In Chapter 4 we'll probe Lewis' theory of front-running more deeply. For now, it is sufficient to say that (a) there is a pretty simple explanation of market-makers getting hoodwinked that explains Thor's initial success, and (b) there is no logical or causal link between Thor's success and a theory of a vast conspiracy of front-running.

---

[16] Lewis writes, "Brad just looked at the guy: He was a young Indian quant." It's never made clear why the ethnicity of the analyst matters.

[17] Some might claim that since market-makers provide a beneficial service to the markets, a tool that takes advantage of them is somewhat unsavory. Having been a market-maker for a long time, I tend to believe that taking it on the chin is part of the business. Also, some portion of the increased costs from things like Thor are passed on to other investors through a wider bid-offer spread.

Estimating the "Tax" of High-Frequency Trading

You have to read the section on Thor and Citigroup a few times before you realize what just happened. The development of Thor (somehow) led to a theory that the price impact of Katsuyama's large trades was due to someone front-running him, and not, well, price impact. Lewis next explains that Katsuyama's team estimated the cost of this alleged front-running based on a single trade of Citigroup shares — how they estimated this when Katsuyama admits that "I just didn't know how they were doing it" is a mystery.[18] By the end of the paragraph, it is assumed that every trade in the market is being front-run. If you blinked, you missed it.

The extrapolation from one trade to the entire U.S. stock market, which then becomes accepted fact for the remaining 200-plus pages of the book, is buried in the math:

> "[The tax of 0.07%] sounded small until you realize that the average daily volume in the U.S. stock market was $225 billion. The same tax rate applied to that sum came to more than $160 million a day."

From this point onward, *Flash Boys* never looks back: it is assumed that every trade in the stock market is being front-run.

Not so fast. As Lewis admits in the paragraphs preceding this estimate, retail stock orders (that's the stock orders that you and I send through E*Trade, Charles Schwab, TD Ameritrade, or whoever your online broker is), are, surprisingly, executed outside the public exchanges on which he alleges this fraud is occurring. So this doesn't apply to the "retail" stock orders you might place through your broker.

---

[18] On the other hand, they were selling a tool to combat this purported scam, so they had to come up with some number. A larger number wouldn't hurt sales.

I suppose you could stop reading at that point since your personal interests are not at stake, but please don't. As Lewis and Katsuyama point out, you may still be affected since public exchanges sometimes execute orders for mutual funds (in which you may be invested) and hedge funds (curiously lumped in by Lewis with "ordinary investors," which is only true for ordinary investors with a minimum net worth of $1 million).

More broadly, the SEC estimates that an additional 17% of market volume is executed directly between large institutions or by retail over-the-counter market-makers, completely outside the reach of high-frequency traders or anyone else.

Lastly, Lewis doesn't claim, nor would it make sense to claim, that high-frequency traders are front-running high-frequency traders. There goes another 50% of the market, at least.

In sum, I don't know how or why Lewis extrapolates from the questionable analysis of a single trade to the entire market, but it clearly isn't sound. The extrapolation appears as flimsy as the premise itself. When I first heard Lewis say on his press tour that, "The market is rigged," I thought he had found another Enron or Bernie Madoff, sending legions of unsuspecting investors to the poor house. I didn't expect to find that, based on a single trade and a few hunches, some old-school big-bank traders speculated that 0.07% of their trades' potential value was going to another subset of traders using questionable practices. If it turned out to be true, it's still unethical and wrong. But it's simply absurd to claim that this would apply to every share traded in the stock market.

And what if the "tax" isn't a tax at all? What if high-frequency trading lowers costs instead of increasing them? As we'll see in Chapter 4, the computerization of the markets wrought by high-frequency traders have reduced transaction costs dramatically in the past ten to fifteen years – by at least 0.50% of invested value. These estimates are not based on someone's invalid extrapolation from a single trade, but rather are the result of comprehensive analyses of market-wide volume.[19] Using this data and Lewis' value for daily market volume, one would find a *tax **rebate** of $1.1 billion per day*. If these markets are rigged, they are rigged in the investor's favor.

Or, ask the broker who handles more retail trades online than anyone else. As TD Ameritrade's CEO Fred Tomczyk sums it up, "The retail investor is better off today than they've ever been in history. Their transaction costs are down probably 80% in the last ten years."[20]

---

[19] For example, see Letter from Gus Sauter, Managing Director and Chief Investment Officer, The Vanguard Group, to the Securities and Exchange Commission, dated April 21, 2010.

[20] See "Milken: Retail investor better off than ever – TD Ameritrade," Reuters, April 29, 2014.

CHAPTER 3:

TRYING TO CONNECT THE DOTS

Co-location

Ronan Ryan's experience at Radianz rings true. As he was plugging in network connections for electronic trading firms, I'm not surprised that he saw gauze wrapped around a co-location cage, or someone leaving Toys "R" Us signs up. There are at least two reasons folks tried to conceal their computer hardware from prying eyes: first, as mentioned earlier, the barriers to entry for electronic trading are ridiculously low and any advantage is significant; second, as demonstrated, guys like Ronan Ryan love to yak about the strange things they've seen, so new innovations don't stay under wraps for long. Incidentally, paranoia has always been the norm everywhere on Wall Street. Hedge funds are constantly fretting that somebody will hear about their great strategy and replicate it, because it's not that hard to do so.

That said, there are a lot of ridiculous things that people have tried for advantage, and it's fun for Ryan to catalog them for us. For example, trimming three feet off a network cable saves about 3 nanoseconds – about the time it takes a computer program to do, well, almost nothing.[21] It's the equivalent of being on a diet and

---

[21] This is six clock cycles on a 2GHz server, for the technically minded.

deciding to eat one fewer cornflake each day at breakfast. The sort of tweaks mentioned by Ryan don't imply hugely profitable evil geniuses to me. They imply a couple of guys getting lucky with some strategy, and not really having any clue as to why they are successful. As Ryan sums it up, "If you know how to pickpocket someone and you were the pickpocketer, you would do the same thing."[22]

Lewis tells us that Ryan became the "world's authority on co-location." While this might be a stretch – I haven't spoken to anyone who had heard of him before *Flash Boys*; he never actually worked at a trading firm; and Katsuyama admits that Ryan didn't know the difference between a bid and an offer — Ryan offers a convenient literary vehicle for Lewis to explore co-location.

Almost all business computers today are co-located in data centers. The data centers provide constant power, 24-hour-a-day monitoring, and security, among other benefits. As network latency began to matter to traders a decade ago, they started to select data centers closer to the exchanges to reduce the time that their data spent in transit, much like Amazon builds local warehouses in major cities across the country to reduce shipping times. As the exchanges modernized and started to move their servers to data centers, they realized that (a) traders want to locate as close as possible to the exchanges to minimize latency, and (b) the exchanges could charge for this co-location privilege.

They did not, as Lewis claims, "[pick] places to set up exchanges so that the market would fragment." Why on earth would an exchange want to encourage fragmentation and send business elsewhere? The motivations were pure business: profit and cost. For example, Lewis writes, "In Australia [the data center] was mysteriously located not in the Sydney financial district but across Sydney Harbor." This isn't really a mystery if you look at real estate prices in the financial district – some of the highest in the world. It's much cheaper a few kilometers away. Lewis asks why so many

---

[22] I have no idea what this phrase actually means.

exchanges are located in New Jersey. The answer is that it's a lot cheaper than Manhattan. Why pay Manhattan rent for a bunch of computers?

Exchange co-location has never been a secret. The service is available to all, and the details are published on exchange websites. The topic has been widely discussed in the financial media and industry for years. When the SEC requested public comments on additional regulation of co-location in January 2010, hundreds responded. Further, since early 2010 the exchanges have submitted their proposed co-location policies and fees to the SEC, which posts them on the SEC website for public comment. While Lewis implies that co-location is some insider secret – "[Ryan] met with hundreds of people. And no one knew about it" – it sounds more like the folks he met with were just clueless.[23]

For most people, the real question behind co-location is whether or not it is fair. The answer is somewhat unsatisfying: it's more fair than the alternative.

Exchange co-location is regulated by the SEC, and, as such, is required to be available to all market participants.[24] Whether or not one thinks it is currently regulated perfectly, it is regulated – thereby providing, if not a guarantee, at least a possibility of fairness. In an exchange data center, the data is broadcast to all traders simultaneously, providing everyone with an equal footing and a fair chance. If exchange co-location were prohibited, traders would still vie to be next to the exchanges. They would just be housed in private data centers, outside the reach of the SEC. Such facilities could discriminate on pricing, or simply establish a monopoly. Any chance at regulation, or fairness, is gone. There would no longer be a

---

[23] In fairness, they might have worked in some other corner of the financial industry (e.g. insurance, or credit card processing) that was unrelated to the equity markets.

[24] Per the SEC, "The terms of co-location services must not be unfairly discriminatory, and the fees must be equitably allocated and reasonable." See SEC Release No. 34-61358, January 14, 2010.

common starting line, but instead a system where, unlike today, some firms actually do get a head start. Further, prohibition of co-location would impact the exchanges' bottom line. Like it or not, this is a profit center for exchanges, subsidized by professional traders. If the subsidy disappears, costs rise for everyone else.

On the plus side, co-location decreases latency for market-makers. This means less risk that the market moves against them unexpectedly, and the reduced risk permits them to make more efficient markets for investors, resulting in a lower cost to buy and sell stock. From the exchanges' perspective, there is also less risk that a participant becomes disconnected from the exchange due to an external network failure.[25]

Philosophically, though, should some market participants be allowed to receive and process data before others? Again, the answer is unsatisfying: the best we can do is to create a fair starting line by broadcasting market data simultaneously to all participants, but we can't control who wins the race. Whether you provide co-location, coil thirty-eight miles of cable as IEX ultimately does, or force participants to connect from across the country, once people receive the data some will react more quickly than others, and we can't legislate the tools they may use or speed in which they may react.

Mike Gitlin, the former Head of Global Trading for T. Rowe Price whom Lewis quotes extensively in this chapter in support of Katsuyama, made exactly this point when he wrote to the SEC in 2010:

> "It is simply not economically feasible to suggest that an individual investor must have equal trading technology and capabilities as that of an investment manager with billions of client dollars under management...It is not clear to us that a

---

[25] When this happens, chaos ensues. Basically, the broker has no idea what trades they have made and what orders are still in the market. If you think that managing the risk in a portfolio is difficult, imagine how hard it is when you don't even know what the portfolio is.

smaller institution or individual investor would benefit from such tools to execute their orders."[26]

Put another way, every investor uses the tools that are appropriate for their goals. The tools employed don't have to be the same for everyone – a long-term investor might choose to spend their money on better research instead of faster computers – but they do have to be equally available to everyone to be fair.

Ultimately, it's quite possible that co-location will be sacrificed on the altar of political expediency, burying the debate. Things will be less fair, and the markets somewhat less efficient, but at least nobody would bother the regulators about the issue any more. I'm skeptical that this would be an improvement.

---

[26] See Letter from Michael Gitlin, Head of Global Trading, T. Rowe Price Associates, Inc., to the Securities and Exchange Commission, dated April 21, 2010. The letter also notes that T. Rowe Price had $391.3 billion in assets under management when Gitlin worked in trading. It's not clear why Lewis chose to inflate this sum to "$700 billion in U.S. stock market investments" – aside from the numbers not matching, Lewis should know that "assets under management" includes cash, bonds, personal stock investments, and many other non U.S. stock market investments.

Front-running: What is it?

Finally, Lewis treats us to a picture of how the high-frequency traders allegedly front-run the entire stock market. Note that we still do not hear from anyone who has ever been a high-frequency trader. Perhaps for Lewis that's not necessary – he has now promoted our protagonists to "the foremost electronic trading expert in the world" and "the world's authority on the subject [of co-location]."

Although these newly bestowed titles are undoubtedly made to bolster his lead characters' credibility, it really strains the reader's credulity: can somebody really be the world's foremost expert in something he has never done? Can somebody really be the world's foremost expert in a field without ever speaking to anyone in that field? Apparently, for Lewis, the answer is yes. Without a lick of experience, then, he proceeds to describe how he believes electronic trading is one vast scam of front-running.

First, what is front-running? Front-running is when a broker receives an order from a customer, and, knowing all the details of the order, "runs" in "front" of the customer's order to execute a similar order for the broker's own account, and then turns around and sells those shares back to the customer at a higher price for a profit. For example, imagine I asked my broker to sell 200 shares of IBM, and my broker immediately went and sold an identical quantity of shares for himself in the market. Now my broker buys those shares back from me, but at a lower price than he received. He takes home a tidy profit, and I, the customer, am none the wiser. This is, quite obviously, illegal.

Fortunately, any would-be front-runner has to overcome at least five hurdles to rip you off:

1) Determine the price and quantity of shares of your order
2) Buy the same amount of shares you want, before you do
3) Manipulate the market price upward

4) Sell the shares back to you at the higher price
5) Avoid anyone else in the market who could disrupt the scam

Despite these hurdles, cases of front-running occurred often thirty years ago, enabled by various flaws in market structure. For example, customer and proprietary orders flowed through the same trading desks at a handful of brokers. It wasn't that hard for the brokers' proprietary traders to learn the price and quantity of customer orders. Executing orders was a slow, cumbersome, and often manual process, providing an unscrupulous broker with plenty of time for shenanigans. Further, brokers had incredible latitude in pricing customer orders – customers could get prices that were significantly worse than the actual market prices – and so the brokers didn't have to explicitly manipulate the market price. They could simply sell the shares back to you at the price they chose. Since the whole transaction occurred away from the markets (or on a market with only a single "specialist" who set the price), the thief didn't have to worry about anyone else disrupting his scam.

Today, things are different. With the electronification of the markets last decade and the implementation of Regulation NMS in 2007, the five hurdles above have now become solid barriers to front-running. As a preliminary matter, the high-frequency trading firms that account for the majority of market activity today operate without any customers. It's hard to sneak a peek at customer orders when you have no customers. When a broker who actually has customers sends a customer order to the markets, this is how it is protected:

> Barrier 1) All order information is hidden from the markets unless the customer chooses otherwise. Even after a trade occurs, nobody except the customer knows the contents of their order. Without the order's price and quantity information, front-running simply isn't possible – a would-be front-runner couldn't know what to front-run.

<u>Barrier 2)</u> Stock exchanges automatically and immediately execute marketable orders. It's impossible for a would-be front runner to buy shares before you do when your order executes automatically and immediately.

<u>Barrier 3)</u> Brokers can no longer stick customers with any price they choose: customer orders are required to execute at the best prices in the markets. Intense competition from a wide variety of firms keeps these market prices incredibly tight, and ensures that no single firm has a monopoly on setting the price a customer receives.

<u>Barriers 4 and 5)</u> The competition in the public markets makes it extremely difficult for a would-be front-runner to ever sell shares back to you and complete the scam – there are already tens of other firms vying to sell shares to the general public at the same price, or better.

It's no coincidence that today's markets present significant barriers to front-running: that's how they were designed in Regulation NMS.

Deeply embedded in modern market structure are the two principles of minimal information disclosure and constrained pricing. Together, they make most would-be scams dead-on-arrival. It's hard to front-run an order if you have no information about it. It's hard to profit from any scam when all of your trades have to occur at the same price that the customer's order does. This is why Lewis' examples of alleged front-running fall apart. To make his examples work he has to violate these principles, and the markets simply don't work that way.

Latency Tables: How to Front-Run. Or Not.

In fact, Lewis concedes that what he alleges isn't actually front-running.[27] He can't realistically get around the issue that there is no communication of customer orders to the alleged perpetrators, intentionally or otherwise. Instead, he alleges that predators somehow infer the order's properties through other mysterious means.

What are these mysterious means that enable high-frequency traders to divine private order information? Lewis tells us that, somehow, this highly paranoid and secretive cabal let down its guard and spilled the beans to Ronan Ryan:

> "Ronan had noticed the HFT guys creating elaborate tables of the time, measured in microseconds, it took for a stock market order to travel from any given brokerage house to each of the exchanges. 'Latency tables,' these are called...They enabled high-frequency traders to identify brokers by the time their orders took to travel from one exchange to the other. Once you had figured out which broker was behind any given stock market order, you could discern patterns in each broker's behavior...You might also guess how the broker might distribute the order among the various exchanges and how much above the current market price for Intel shares the broker might be willing to pay."

Let us recall two facts from the development of Thor, shared a few pages prior. First, they started by "estimating the differences in travel time it took to send the messages to the various exchanges, and by building the equivalent delays into their software." Second, "the travel times were never the same...because the paths the electronic signals took from Brad's desk to the various exchanges

---

[27] Regardless of its inaccuracy, we'll use Lewis' term "front-running" for the sake of continuity.

were inconsistent." We'll come back to the first point in a bit, but let's talk about inconsistent travel times.

This inconsistency means that building a "latency table" to identify RBC orders in the market would have been pointless since the travel times of RBC orders were essentially random – Lewis himself gives an example where one order takes almost twice as long as the prior order. That bears repeating: unless a broker has custom-built its own fiber network, a "latency table" would be worthless. In other words, if Katsuyama was being front-run at that time, it couldn't have been this way.

For the sake of argument, though, assume that all other brokers on Wall Street had custom-built fiber network paths that delivered consistent, predictable latency (a rather unreasonable assumption since (a) it was a significant cost, and (b) Ronan required stolen telecom maps to create his custom network). Then the HFT guys just watch for orders labeled "RBC" and measure when they arrive at each exchange, right? Not quite – the orders have to go to the exchanges based on which exchanges have the best price, not based on a chart at the broker. And there are of course hundreds of different traders and trading algorithms at each broker, each of which may have different ideas about which exchange to send his order to, and when. All of these decisions are based on the broker's view of the market data, which is unique to that broker and their systems. But the clever HFT guys have nuclear physicists who can tease this data out of all the noise, right? Maybe they use "data mining" or other fancy analysis? No, and no. The last problem is that neither orders nor trades ever identify the source. No order is ever labeled "RBC." No completed trades are labeled "RBC." Thus, there's no way to connect an order or trade to a broker – before, during, or after a trade – and thus no data to data-mine. So even if the network latencies weren't completely random, it still would be impossible to create "latency tables" for other brokers.

And even if it were possible, it wouldn't be useful. If one had a set of perfect latency tables for all algorithms used by all traders at every broker in the market, and all brokers had non-random, precise and unique latencies, one would still never have enough data to figure out who sent an order. Contrary to what Lewis implies, it is utterly impossible to identify anything from a single order on the BATS Exchange. One moment there is nothing. The next moment there is a trade. Nobody knows how long it took the order to hit the BATS Exchange, they only know that a single trade occurred.

The next trade on the next exchange isn't going to be terribly helpful either. One could conceivably measure the difference in time between the trades, but it's basically useless in identifying anyone since that difference would provide a *single data point*. Perhaps by the third or fourth exchange one could narrow the field of possible brokers and trading algorithms a bit, but by that time the trade is complete. Remember that all these orders were already in transit anyway, so the whole exercise was pointless to begin with – by the time you saw the first trade report come back, the other orders would be long gone.

Amusingly, the other example Lewis uses to illustrate this theory is a trading algorithm that purchases 100,000 shares, "[buying] 5,000 shares every five minutes, so long as the price is no higher than $25." Not only would a "latency table" not provide perfect information, it would provide no information at all – the trades are occurring minutes apart.

Lastly, Lewis completely dodges the question of how any of this nonsense would ever reveal the actual quantity and price of an order. Without this information, there's no front-running possible.

In the end, I suspect that what Ryan thinks he saw at high-frequency trading firms was not a front-running tool for prophesying the existence of a particular broker's order – a problem that is simultaneously impossible to solve and useless to solve. It was simply an internal table of latencies for these firms' *own* order routing to each exchange. There are legitimate reasons to build latency tables that have nothing to do with conspiracies. In fact,

Lewis describes RBC compiling just such a table of latencies for Thor – not to foretell the existence of somebody else's order, but rather to efficiently route an order for immediate execution. That would be useful. And doable.

Front-running: Bad for Business. Or Just Bad Business?

Lewis makes one last try at illustrating how his front-running scam would work, abandoning latency tables in favor of the more vague idea that "[t]he brokers' routers, like bad poker players, all had a conspicuous tell":

> "...you wish to buy 100,000 shares of Company XYZ at $25, 10,000 on each of ten different exchanges, all of which will charge the broker to trade on your behalf (though far less than the commission you have paid to him). There are, however, another 100 shares for sale, also at $25, on the BATS exchange – which will pay the broker for the trade. The sequential cost-effective router will go first to BATS and buy the 100 shares – and cause the other 100,000 shares to vanish into the paws of high-frequency traders (in the bargain relieving the broker of the obligation to pay to trade). The high-frequency traders can then turn around and sell the shares of Company XYZ at a higher price, or hold onto the shares for a few seconds more, while you, the investor, chase Company XYZ's shares even higher."

This creative hypothetical should frighten any investor: these guys can tell from a single 100-share trade that there is an order for 99,900 more shares on the way? Of course they can't.

The idea of a "broker's tell" is Lewis' last ditch effort to explain without explaining. Sometimes critics instead choose to say high-frequency traders use "artificial intelligence" or "machine learning" to obtain omniscience, but, whatever the turn of phrase, it just boils down to a retreat to vague hand-waving.

Nobody knows the size of the new order. Lewis' whole scam hinges on this assumption that the "front-runners" have perfect knowledge of an order. But even if we assume that through latency tables (already debunked) or "router tells" somebody can divine where the next part of an order would go, how can they tell whether or not there even will be another part of the order?

When 100 shares trade on BATS, the only information available to anyone is that 100 shares just traded on BATS. To claim that anyone, based on this information, can divine whether zero additional shares were desired or 99,900 additional shares were desired is pure fantasy. Period.

However, for the sake of argument, let's indulge Lewis' rhetorical fantasy: imagine the front-runners somehow did guess that more shares are coming. How many? 1,000? 2,000? 99,000? To get those shares immediately they will have to pay trading fees for taking liquidity, usually $0.003 per share. It doesn't bode well for them that their would-be scam starts with a built-in loss. If they guessed the wrong quantity – say, this was actually an order for a total of 100 shares, not 100,000 shares – they will soon have to "cross the spread" to unwind their failed wager, paying at least a penny plus more trading fees. In total, an incorrect guess would cost a minimum of 1.6 cents per share.

That doesn't sound like a big loss, but in Chapter 2, Lewis told us that he estimates the average profit of front-runners is about $0.0029 per share.[28] After accounting for trading fees, their profit

---

[28] Specifically, he said the "tax" was $29,000 on ten million shares of Citigroup, or $0.0029 per share. While this is, coincidentally, almost precisely the amount that an exchange charges per share traded, I'm assuming that his analysis didn't mistakenly include trading fees (doing so would make the "tax" zero).

would be more like $0.0019 per share.[29] (In reality, their trading profits are less than half this). So if these front-runners guess the quantity incorrectly, they lose at least *eight times more* than they could make. When Lewis says that high-frequency traders "only needed to skew the odds systematically in their favor," this can't be what he meant.[30]

Actually, the odds are even worse for the front-runner. If there are many front-runners, as Lewis alleges, then the odds of losing increase dramatically: what if ten different predators each go out to buy 100,000 more shares? Even if they all guessed the correct quantity of the original order, at least 90% of their activity will be money-losing.

Guessing the order's size wouldn't help. Aiming for smaller quantities to avoid hemorrhaging money on excess shares won't work either. The average trade size in the public markets is less than 200 shares, and the median trade size is smaller still.[31] Suppose the front-runner guesses that every 100-share trade on BATS portends another 100 shares somewhere else. Obviously this approach doesn't square with Lewis' idea that they are front-running large orders, but since this is the only remaining theory that might not lose money for the front-runner, let's consider it. Unfortunately for them, they will still be wrong more than half the time. With eight to one

---

[29] In Lewis' front-running scam, they would pay $0.0030 per share to buy these shares initially. I assume (somewhat improbably) that they are lucky enough to offset this fee partially with a $0.0020 per share rebate when selling the shares back. For simplicity's sake I ignore SEC, FINRA, and NSCC per-trade fees, which further reduce a would-be front-runner's profits.

[30] One could also interpret Lewis' front-running estimate of $0.0029 per share as a profit of one penny (less trading fees) 29% of the time, and a "miss" / loss for the other 71% of the time. The results would be similar: the front-runners lose twice as often as they would win, and each loss is almost twice as big as any "win."

[31] See "As Odd-Lots Report to Tape, Average Trade Size Declines Again," Gary Stone and Sanghuyn Park, Bloomberg Tradebook, March 4, 2014.

odds, being wrong just half the time costs a lot of money – eight dollars lost per dollar gained.

In sum, there simply isn't any way that a front-runner could be in a winning position.

Manipulating the price. While Lewis waves his hand and says that the front-runner sells the shares back at a higher price, it's not that simple. How do they move the market to that "higher price"?

By law, nobody can trade at a higher price until every single offer in the market at the lower price is gone. The only way to get rid of somebody else's lower offers is to buy them up. So, in Lewis' scam, the front-runner has to buy *every single share in every single market* that is offered at the current price. If there are one million shares of XYZ offered at $25.01, the front-runner would have to buy every single one of them before he could turn around and sell your 100,000 shares back to you at the higher price of $25.02. This premise is utterly absurd. If it were true, every time a new order for 100 shares hit the market, the front-runners would have to purchase every single share available at the current price. Within a few minutes, they would own millions of shares – and they'd have to unload them for a serious loss.

Selling the shares back. If, miraculously, the would-be front-runner successfully manipulated the price higher, it wouldn't be easy for him to sell a single share at the new, higher price. There were lots of other folks in the market who already offered to sell shares of XYZ before this fiasco, and the front-runner would have to go to the back of the line to sell his shares. Then he has to wait patiently for his turn. It will probably be a long time. As you'd expect, there are always many more people willing to sell at a higher price than the current best price, so the number of shares already offered at $25.02

would be significant. And the front-runner can't sell a single share until every share that was there before him has been sold.

During that time, the market may rise, in which case his resting offer trades, capturing a one-penny profit. On the other hand, the market may fall, in which case he doesn't sell his shares, his small potential profit turns to a much larger loss, and he still has to figure out how to get out of a losing trade. Due to a phenomenon known as "mean reversion," which is a fancy way of saying things tend to return to normal – particularly if there was no fundamental reason for the price to change – it's more likely that the market will settle back to the original price, and the front-runner is stuck with that large loss. Don't forget, the loss would be on a position that could be ten times larger than the order he was trying to front-run in the first place.

In sum, even if a front-runner accurately guessed the quantity of an order (which is well nigh impossible), and they fended off all competitors (admittedly, I have no idea how this would happen), they are more likely than not to be stuck with a massive losing position as their reward.

Again, this doesn't sound like a very good business model.

The Illogic of Predictability. Lastly, one has to ask the most obvious question of all: if you know exactly what these front-runners are doing, why can't you beat them? Or at least avoid them? If you want to buy 100,000 shares of XYZ, why not play the opposite game of the high-frequency traders: quietly place resting bids to purchase the shares on those ten exchanges first, and then wait for somebody to sell 100 shares of XYZ on BATS, causing your 100,000 resting shares to be the ones that "vanish into the paws of high-frequency traders?" As a bonus, you even collect a rebate from the exchange on the 100,000 shares.

Reading the book alternate between the victimization of Katsuyama's traders and their explanation of exactly how they are being victimized, I feel like I'm hearing somebody complain that they always lose playing rock-paper-scissors: they always choose rock and the other guy always chooses paper. Why not choose scissors?

More broadly, if these front-runners are running this scam all the time, not only should Katsuyama be able to avoid it, other predators would likely front-run the front-runners, putting them out of business. Lewis tells us that Brad describes this front-running plague to everyone on Wall Street, including a number of sharp hedge fund managers. Did all of these hedge funds decide to play nice with the high-frequency front-runners? Have all the other high-frequency traders, whom he claims make money picking off predictable models, decided not to pick off these guys who predictably front-run? It just doesn't sound plausible.

One suspects that Lewis would sidestep the logical contradiction at the heart of *Flash Boys* by saying that it's really more complicated than he makes it in the book. I'd agree.

Are there predators in the market that are looking to pick off an errant trade? I'd say so – that's what many day traders do, that's what many hedge funds do, and that's probably what some computers do too. Does this imply that there is a vast conspiracy of front-running covering 50% of the market? No. The math doesn't work, and the logic doesn't work.

Still, the theory provides comfort to those who would rather blame someone else than sift through messy details to figure out why their trade went south. And it makes for a great sales pitch for Thor.

The Market Behaves Unexpectedly (again again): The Case of the China ETF

Take the next example, of a hedge fund president to whom Katsuyama has just pitched the Thor / front-running conspiracy theory:

> "[The hedge fund president] sat at his desk watching both his personal online brokerage account and his $1,800-a-month Bloomberg terminal. In his private brokerage account he set out to buy an exchange-traded fund (ETF) comprised of Chinese construction companies. Over several hours he watched the price of the fund on his Bloomberg terminal. It was midnight in China, nothing was happening, and the ETF's price didn't budge. He then clicked the Buy button on his online brokerage account screen, and the price on the Bloomberg screen jumped. Most people who used online brokerage accounts didn't have Bloomberg terminals that enabled them to monitor the market in something close to real time. Most investors never knew what happened in the market after they pressed the Buy button. "I hadn't even hit Execute," says the hedge fund president. "I hadn't done anything but put in a ticker symbol and a quantity to buy. And the market popped."

This does sound suspicious. How likely is it that the market changed just as our hedge fund manager started to enter his order? As the hedge fund manager noted, it was midnight in China. Why would the stock price change?

The answer is actually quite simple. When the U.S. stock market rises, markets around the world tend to rise, and when the U.S. stock market falls, markets around the world tend to fall, including China. Hedge fund managers even have a name for this relationship: "beta." For example, the "beta" of GXC, an ETF comprised of Chinese companies, is 1.17. This means that if the U.S. stock market rises 1%, this China ETF rises 1.17%; if the U.S. market falls by 1%, this

Chinese ETF falls by 1.17%. If it's midnight in China, it is noon in New York and the U.S. markets are moving, swinging up and down and taking this China ETF with them. Given this fact, it would only be suspicious if the China ETF did *not* change price when the U.S. market was open.

But Wall Street's professionals are a curiously superstitious lot. We often imagine hedge fund managers making hard-nosed decisions solely on the basis of rigorous mathematical models fueled by mountains of financial data, and for some, this is true. But watch a few minutes of CNBC and you'll quickly see people entrusted with billions of dollars debating the predictive powers of the "Hindenburg Omen" versus the "Golden Cross" – with a surprising amount of confidence and conviction. If it seems unbelievable, it helps to consider how many people would invest in a money manager if he admitted, "I have no clue why the market dropped yesterday and I have even less of an idea what tomorrow will bring." All of this is to say that while it seems surprising that the hedge fund president in Lewis' story ignored such an obvious explanation as the beta relationship, it's not. That's Wall Street.[32]

For the sake of argument, however, let us go along with the implausible idea that the movement of the China ETF wasn't connected to the broader market. Perhaps the entire U.S. market itself was, remarkably, utterly quiet for all of the "several hours" of this hedge fund manager's experiment. Let us also go along with the idea that something sinister caused the market to "pop" after the hedge fund president entered his ticker symbol and quantity, but before he hit "Execute." If true, this would be far more sinister than Lewis has even imagined – for somehow, the pack of predatory high-

---

[32] Lewis tells us that this hedge fund president also apparently has "a three-hundred million-dollar problem in a nine-billion-dollar hedge fund" caused by "not being able to trade at the stated market prices." This cost amounts to 3.3% of his total portfolio, an estimate 45 times higher than Lewis' estimate of the "tax" of high-frequency trading in Chapter 2. It sounds like this hedge fund has many problems. I don't think they are related to high-frequency trading.

frequency traders lying in wait had divined the hedge fund president's order *before he had even sent it from his computer.* Pause a moment and consider this: the order is not sent onto the network until he hits "Execute," and the price moves *before* he hits "Execute." Lewis is telling us that the markets reacted before the order ever left his PC.

If the order has not yet been sent anywhere, by what means do these high-frequency traders prophesy its existence? Are they secretly watching that very PC in his office? Or are their models are so sophisticated that from afar they could predict that this hedge fund manager would perform this China ETF experiment on this day, at this very millisecond?

As I pondered the impossibility of it, I weighed other scenarios where Lewis may have forgotten a key detail. Perhaps this was a limit order that rested in the market, and this caused the market to "pop"? Impossible: Lewis tells us the order was filled at a higher, worse price, and by definition a limit order is filled at the limit price at which it is entered, or a better price if available. Perhaps part of the order filled at the original price on one exchange, and then the hedge funder was front-run as the rest of the order went to other exchanges? Impossible again: the order was filled internally by Citadel Derivatives (who matches many such orders for E*Trade) and never made it to the public markets; furthermore, Lewis tells us that the price moved *before* the order was sent. I've asked experienced traders to review this anecdote, and to assume that super-evil front-runners were lurking at every turn, and asked them: is this possible? The answer is an unequivocal no.

So perhaps a better question is: why, if in 200-plus pages, Lewis is going to put forth only three real-world examples purporting a vast market-wide conspiracy of front-running, would he choose this one? If this was one of the most credible and compelling anecdotes, one wonders what less-believable evidence was edited out.

The Flash Crash Conspiracy Theory

For stock market pundits, the flash crash of May 6, 2010, when the stock market and stock futures markets plunged 6% and recovered only twenty minutes later, is something of a Rorschach test. For data-driven analysts, this was an opportunity to dive deep into the complexity of the derivatives and equities markets, evaluate how they had failed, and fix it. Another group, however, gleefully rubbed their hands together in anticipation of a witch-hunt indulging their favorite conspiracy theory: high-frequency traders gone wild. When the SEC and CFTC issued their joint analysis after five months of investigation, the former group got what it wanted, and a series of market reforms were implemented to prevent a recurrence of the event. The latter group was sorely disappointed in the conclusion – it did not blame high-frequency traders – and quickly dismissed the report out of hand.

Even more infuriating to the conspiracists, the report had actually taken a hard, detailed look at high-frequency trading and didn't find anything. While Katsuyama derides the SEC-CFTC report because the word "millisecond" is only found four times, the phrase "HFT" is found over one hundred times.[33] After spending five months poring over records at every exchange and information subpoenaed from across the industry – including many high-frequency trading firms – shouldn't there be some really juicy tidbits about high-frequency traders in the 104-page report?

Apparently not. Since there was nothing sufficiently scandalous in the report, Lewis denounces it.[34] He mocks the SEC for "blaming

---

[33] I fully recognize that it's absurd to judge any research project on the basis of a word count of the final report. This is akin to dismissing the National Science Foundation's 114-page climate change report because it only mentions "sunspots" twice. My point here is that this absurd analysis cuts both ways.

[34] To be clear, the report analyzed high-frequency traders in substantial depth – they receive twice as much ink than any other category of market

the entire fiasco on a single large sell order, of stock market futures contracts, mistakenly placed on an exchange in Chicago by an obscure Kansas City mutual fund." Lewis' synopsis of the report sounds so absurd that one wonders how the SEC could have come to this conclusion. It didn't.

Briefly, the SEC-CFTC report listed a cascade of events, starting with a highly volatile market that was already in the midst of the biggest one-day drop of that year. The downdraft was then exacerbated by an unusually aggressive series of orders to sell $4.1 billion of a benchmark futures contract. Just as Katsuyama dumping a million shares of Solectron in a jittery merger-arbitrage market caused a "minicollapse," so did this trade. Only this trade wasn't in a tiny tech stock, it was a market-wide product. And just as Thor smacked unlucky market-makers, dumping a lot more risk onto them than they anticipated, so did this trade.

Naturally, the unlucky market-makers who had just bought billions of dollars of stock futures (in the midst of the market's worst day all year) looked to hedge their risk. With the market plunging, however, risk management systems had halted trading for many firms that might take the other side of the trade. At the exchanges, risk management systems kicked in as well, but each behaved in its own way, creating more confusion – some exchanges paused trading, others did not. On top of it all, market data systems started to strain under the panic-driven activity, delivering suspect data and making everything worse. In sum, it was a cascade of problems, each fueling the next one. Regulators have used this analysis to implement solutions for each point in the cascade, hopefully preventing any single future problem from igniting a broader conflagration.

For example, the SEC now legally requires brokers to apply risk controls *before* an order is placed – preventing orders like the one that started the flash crash from crushing the markets. Further, if

---

participant – but didn't find anything remotely supporting Lewis' claims about high-frequency traders front-running or destabilizing the markets.

there is an abrupt drop in a stock, all trading in that stock is paused. If the broader markets fall abruptly, the SEC and CFTC have mandated a uniform market-wide halt to trading.

If you're still curious, please read at least the executive summary of the SEC-CFTC report – it really answers a lot of questions and has a lot of data behind it. If you're not still curious, just know that (a) the SEC and CFTC gathered and synthesized mountains of data to produce a comprehensive report, and (b) important fixes were made after the flash crash to prevent a recurrence in similar volatile markets, although more work still needs to be done.

Does The Data Exist?

"No one could say for sure what caused the flash crash – for the same reason no one could prove that high-frequency traders were front-running the orders of ordinary investors. The data didn't exist."

It may take a while to unpack these three conclusions that Lewis links together. Let us put aside the fact that, in interviews subsequent to the publication of *Flash Boys*, Lewis and Katsuyama all but admitted that this alleged front-running couldn't affect the orders of ordinary investors (contradicting the middle conclusion). Let us also grant that, although there are a lot of pretty good explanations for the flash crash, no one will ever be able to say with 100% certainty what caused it, if for no other reason than the event involved the intentions and decisions of thousands of individuals, whose minds we cannot read. We are still left with the question: does the data exist?

Lewis is correct in saying that the data *to support his claim* does not exist. However, he is utterly incorrect when he says that fine-grained trading data doesn't exist.

For example, Lewis writes, "The unit of trading was now the microsecond, but the records kept by the exchanges were by the second." **This is completely false.** Had Lewis really interviewed anyone at an exchange, he would have been disabused of this notion immediately. Every event that occurs in any given stock at an exchange occurs in a precise order that can be replayed. If order A to buy Microsoft arrives one microsecond before order B to buy Microsoft, it is processed before order B. You can call the exchange and ask what happened, and they can replay the precise sequence, in the exact order that everything occurred. Even ten years ago – when most traders considered the unit of trading to be the second — we would call an exchange and ask what happened at a particular millisecond and get an immediate answer.[35]

But even this misses the point completely. Katsuyama complains that you can't see a "single time-stamped sheet of every trade." This does exist – everyone trading in the market possesses this data. I don't know why he didn't. The SEC pored over many time-stamped sheets of every trade in their investigation of the flash crash. The SEC has also pored over many time-stamped sheets of every trade in probes of high-frequency traders, as well as their source code, emails, and other data. The data is there, and it doesn't support the front-running theory.

This leads to one of the most surprising revelations of the book: none of the allegations of front-running are substantiated by a single shred of market data.

Katsuyama spent years honing his sales-call pitch of a high-frequency front-running conspiracy, yet during all that time he apparently didn't find any supporting market data evidence worth mentioning in this book. Instead, he tries to sell us the bogus excuse that such data doesn't (and can't) exist.

---

[35] Again, for the technically minded, the underlying Unix operating system at the exchanges has kept time in milliseconds since the 1970s. Finer precision has been available and in use for more than a decade.

At every trading firm I've seen, when a trade goes wrong the trader replays the market data to see what happened. They walk through every trade and every order in the market data and figure out what happened. In *Flash Boys*, the reader is simply told that bids or offers "disappeared." If Katsuyama were being front-run as he described, he would see trades occurring immediately ahead of his, at exactly the prices and quantities he was trying to obtain. If no such trades are found, he's not being front-run. He would also see these trades being "flipped" soon thereafter as the alleged front-runners take their profits and exit their position. Any Wall Street intern with a Bloomberg account could figure this out in thirty seconds.[36] So why is the reader not given the answer here, and instead fed the excuse that the data doesn't exist?

When someone investigating a conspiracy theory cannot corroborate the theory, the last-ditch defense of the conspiracy theorist is to claim that the evidence supporting their conspiracy is now impossible to find.

The fact of the matter is that the amount of data available is voluminous: not just trading records, but order records, market data, computer code, emails, instant messages. Regulators can demand this information from any broker at any time – no lengthy court process or subpoena is required. The data does exist, and lots of it.

Oddly, in later chapters Lewis reveals some knowledge of the vast amounts of data available to investigators: John Schwall complains about his brokerage firm recording his email; Sergey Aleynikov talks about using a source control system called subversion, which records each and every change to the computer code used for trading. In fact, every single evening, every single broker-dealer registered with FINRA uploads a record of every single stock order they placed that day, complete with the

---

[36] Admittedly, given the way they've analyzed the data they had, it's not clear that extra data would help them come to more reasonable conclusions.

millisecond that they sent it.[37] That's worth repeating, because it's rather remarkable. Every night, every broker has to submit to the regulators a record of every order they touched that day. There's no chance of destroying or falsifying incriminating evidence: the orders are all cross-checked against the exchange records as soon as they are uploaded.

In short, this means that every piece of evidence necessary to track down a high-frequency trader who is manipulating the markets would be a few clicks away from any regulator. The trades and orders document what happened, the emails and instant messages document why it happened, and the computer code demonstrates how it happened. Consider the wealth of evidence available: in the past, numerous insider trading cases against hedge funds stalled trying to prove the why and how. If any high-frequency trader breaks the law, the computer code demonstrates irrefutably how it was done and exactly why. The emails and instant messages provide the icing on the cake at trial.

Every day, tens of millions of trades occur. If Lewis's front-running theory is even partially right, it implies millions of violations of securities laws every day. It would be almost impossible to avoid stumbling across evidence of the conspiracy. One would expect to see hundreds of cases against high-frequency front-runners. But we don't. Why?

The most reasonable explanation would be that if these crimes are being committed, they are quite rare. For the inveterate conspiracy theorists, however, the only way to dodge this conclusion is by insinuating that the regulators must also be in on the front-running conspiracy – which, if you are keeping count, would now have to include high-frequency traders, big banks, all the stock exchanges, and the regulators. Are we really to believe that every

---

[37] FINRA is the other major regulator overseeing broker-dealers. Many broker-dealers are regulated by both FINRA and the SEC, and thereby enjoy the pleasure of multiple audits from different regulators each year.

one of these groups has sworn to some code of silence? A more reasonable explanation is that (a) front-running is extremely hard to do in today's markets, and (b) the massive amount of surveillance data available deters criminal activity.

It's extremely difficult to front-run in our modern markets. Every would-be explanation of front-running relies on some imagined method for divining the mere existence of a customer order, and Lewis doesn't even try to explain how somebody figures out the number of shares in the order – the one piece of information that is actually needed to make the scam plausible. Even with that information, the economics would be entirely skewed against the front-runner due to the markets' rules on the price and prioritization of trades. Lastly, today's markets are made up of a huge, diverse set of participants. It's absurd to think that a predictable front-running scheme wouldn't either be easily avoided, or be a target itself. Any front-running scam would have to overcome each and every one of these obstacles to succeed – and then, it would have to evade a massive surveillance system built to track every piece of trading data available.

This market surveillance serves as a significant deterrent. When a city installs "red light cameras" that automatically track drivers who violate a red light, fewer people run red lights. Now, imagine one hundred times more surveillance. Imagine that your car's computer tracked every detail of your driving habits – your speed every millisecond on every street, when and where you stopped, whether or not you used your turn signals, with video of who was in the crosswalk, too. Now imagine that the police can stop you at any time and review your car's data to see you if ever exceeded the speed limit or failed to stop at a stop sign. Most people would become much more careful about their driving. In fact, I'd even pay extra for a new car if it could prevent me from speeding or running a red light.

So it is in today's electronic stock markets. On any day, the regulators can show up at your door and demand to see every detail of your trading. If they find anything amiss, you don't just get a ticket, you lose your driver's license – you are no longer allowed to trade. In other words, if you so much as run a red light, you run the risk of shutting down your company and permanently ending your career. It's no surprise that most electronic trading firms spend prodigiously on compliance systems that monitor their own trading to stop somebody who is about to "go for it" on a yellow light. The risk is too high.

The use of computer software itself is also another deterrent. Electronic trading strategies are executed by computer programs. They are the recipes for these strategies. Computers do what they are told to do, nothing more and nothing less. Never before in the history of the markets have any traders had to write down the recipes that state how they are trading and why. Yet electronic trading requires exactly this. If some trading firm really is front-running the markets electronically, it had to write a computer program to do so – and that program is now available to the regulators. How many would-be criminals do you think keep a diary of their exploits, complete with instructions on how it's done? Given the amount of surveillance, the odds are heavily against anyone who tries to manipulate the markets electronically.

Is it possible that some drivers will still run a red light, even if they know that they are guaranteed to be convicted if they get caught? Yes. Sadly, in any walk of life there will be those who break the rules. Some of those people will break the rules the old fashioned way, and some will now use computers to do their dirty work. Fortunately, in the surveillance state that is today's stock market, such a violation would have to be pretty rare and pretty insignificant to avoid detection.

Finding Proof (of something): CBSX Volume and Spread Networks

The story Lewis tells about CBSX is a relatively small anecdote, but it neatly demonstrates both a conspiracy paranoia and a lack of real trading knowledge.

As Lewis correctly notes, the Chicago-based CBOE Stock Exchange (CBSX) suddenly exploded with activity in late 2010 – specifically, trading in the stock of Sirius. Why? Katsuyama and Ryan put their heads together and figured out that it must be because Spread Networks' new fiber-optic cable between Chicago and New York just became operational, yet again somehow proving in their minds that high-frequency traders were front-running the market through speed. What this really proves is that they still didn't understand a thing about electronic trading in 2010.

Recall that in Chapter 1, Lewis tells us that there were billions to be made trading "Thing A" and "Thing B" between New York and Chicago. Lewis never tells us what Thing A and Thing B were, possibly because it might spoil this anecdote later in the book. Here are two possibilities: (1) Thing A is the CME's eMini S&P 500 future contract, worth about $55,000 per contract in 2010, and Thing B is SPY, the S&P 500 ETF and single-most heavily traded stock, or (2) Thing A is the "SIRI," the common stock of Sirius Corp, worth about $1.10 per share in 2010, and Thing B is the same, identical common stock as Thing A. Which do you think is the billion-dollar opportunity? Hint: it's not Sirius.

The real story is this: CBSX made a brilliant business observation that had nothing to do with geography. As Lewis writes, SIRI traded heavily before CBSX came on the scene. The key was that the low price of SIRI made it an attractive trade. On some days, the highest price that SIRI traded was only *one cent higher* than the lowest price it traded. If the market had a relatively volatile day where it dropped 2%, SIRI would also drop 2% — about two cents. On that same day, Google's stock might drop $5.00 per share. In other words, the low price of SIRI reduced the price risk significantly. If you were willing to buy SIRI for $1.00 and sell it for $1.01, you had much less absolute price risk per share than in any other stock. On many days, the price wouldn't budge, and you could collect a penny buying and selling all day long.

While normally exchanges had to pay a market-maker to stick out their neck, for SIRI the risk in making a market to buy and sell was very low. The folks at CBSX wondered if the lower risk meant higher profits for market-makers. If so, would the market-makers *pay* for the privilege of sticking their neck out? The answer was probably yes, but very few bothered to make markets on the CBSX since nothing traded there. So the ingenious solution was to pay traders to *take* liquidity (who now suddenly got a rebate instead of paying to trade), and to charge the market-makers (who now paid a lot more, but didn't have any choice). In short order, everyone who wanted to take liquidity in SIRI came to CBSX, and it captured a huge market share in that stock. Notably, its market share in higher-priced stocks – where the risk/reward premium was vastly different than SIRI – remained anemic.

Within a few months the other exchanges caught on and changed their pricing accordingly. With the pricing being equivalent, trading volume in SIRI decreased at CBSX and returned to the other exchanges. This story of exchange pricing driving exchange market share is hardly a secret. It was widely known amongst traders, and of course amongst the exchanges that matched CBSX's inverted pricing.[38]

To review, in September 2010 two things happened: CBSX changed pricing, and Spread Networks went live. Volume in SIRI on CBSX jumped. After other exchanges matched the CBSX pricing, and volume in SIRI on CBSX went back to normal. Nothing changed on

---

[38] For example, see "CBSX 'Get Paid to Take' Model – a Glimpse into the Future," Dennis Dick, Tabb Forum, August 23, 2010.

Spread Networks at that time. What is the more plausible explanation?

It's clear that the brief spike in trading volume at CBSX can be explained much better by pricing economics (and corroborated by talking to anyone who traded SIRI at that time), than by a high-frequency conspiracy theory. If the anecdote proves anything, it's not about high-frequency traders, but about how naive some folks are.

There's Only One Thing To Do: Make Money Another Way

> As he put it, "There's a difference between choosing a crusade and having it thrust upon you"...it took him a while to figure out that fate and circumstance had created for him a dramatic role, which he was obliged to play..."It feels like I'm an expert in something that badly needs to be changed. I think there's only a few people in the world who can do anything about this. If I don't do something right now – me, Brad Katsuyama – there's no one to call."

As Lewis tells us in the next sentence (which opens Chapter 4), Katsuyama did do something: he "built a marketable weapon."

CHAPTER 4:

THERE'S ANOTHER EXPLANATION, BUT IT'S NOT AS INTERESTING

"About [high-frequency traders] they knew surprisingly little. Apart from Ronan, Brad knew no one from inside the world of high-frequency trading."

Regulation NMS

Lewis opens his discussion of Regulation NMS by posing the question, "How was it legal for a handful of insiders to operate at faster speeds than the rest of the market, and, in effect, steal from investors?" Here Lewis moves from the more specific allegation of theft through front-running to a more general premise that operating at "faster speeds than the rest of the market" is tantamount to "steal[ing] from investors." This is quite a leap of logic. Personally, I don't like it either that some people are faster than I am. By the time I've had breakfast, checked the news, and planned a trade, sometimes the market has been open for an hour or more. While I wish everyone had waited for me to arrive before commencing trading that morning, I hesitate to call everybody else a thief for doing so.

Lewis portrays the implementation of Regulation NMS in 2007 as the watershed moment that unleashed the high-frequency front-running conspiracy: "The regulation also made it far easier for high-frequency traders to predict where brokers would send their customers' orders, as they must send them first to the exchange that offered the best price." (Credit to Lewis, this sentence demonstrates consummate skill turning a phrase: he makes it sound incredibly sinister that, after decades of ripping off their own customers, brokers are now required by law to obtain the best price possible for their customers.)

The idea that Regulation NMS birthed high-frequency trading might be more believable if it were true high-frequency trading only emerged after 2007. This isn't the case. Just a few pages later – after he has moved on from blaming Regulation NMS for enabling high-frequency trading – Lewis admits that, "In 2005 a quarter of all trades in the public stock markets were made by HFT firms." If Regulation NMS bestowed the ability to front-run upon high-frequency traders, what were they doing before Regulation NMS arrived?

Had Lewis spoken to anyone at any of the largest high-frequency trading firms, he not only would have learned that they were all operational long before Regulation NMS. He also would have learned that they trade in many other markets – currencies, bonds, futures, options, commodities to name a few – where Regulation NMS doesn't apply. They didn't spring into being because of Regulation NMS, and likewise their success doesn't spring from Regulation NMS either.

Some of the other markets these firms trade upon have only one single exchange; many lack co-location; some are archaic and slow; many more have no concept of maker-taker pricing. In fact, if one scans the information publicly available about these high-frequency trading firms, it becomes clear that the U.S. equities market is a mere fraction of their business.[39] As it turns out, the majority of their

---

[39] For example, go online to read the publicly available annual report of Getco/KCG, one of the market's largest high-frequency traders, or any of the many disclosure statements they have filed with the SEC.

trading doesn't depend upon Regulation NMS, maker-taker pricing, or many of the things that Lewis describes as the foundations of "rigged" markets.

It's quite interesting when you consider it. The argument is that high-frequency trading is bad, and we can fix this if we eliminate co-location, maker-taker pricing, and Regulation NMS's best execution requirements. But apparently none of these items are necessary for high-frequency trading. If they were eliminated, high-frequency trading would still exist. The only difference would be that big bank equity traders like Katsuyama and friends would have much lower costs (no co-location necessary, much lower trading fees) and much more discretion in obtaining "best execution" for their clients.

The real reason that Regulation NMS requires "best execution" is that Wall Street brokers abused their fiduciary responsibilities in the past: brokers took advantage of client orders by giving them inferior prices to the market, and pocketing the difference. Regulation NMS's requirement that customers get the best price in the markets didn't enable high-frequency front-running, it enabled customers to finally get the best price in the markets. Sadly, while Regulation NMS cut off one form of abuse, Wall Street's old guard still finds ways to skim from individual investors: unleash your inner John Schwall and Google "soft dollar abuses."

The SIP is Awful and Causes Many Problems, But Not This One

Lewis later concedes that Regulation NMS's best execution standard "would have been fine," but for its reliance upon the Securities Information Processor (SIP). The SIP is a service that provides a picture of the best-priced bids and best-priced offers in the national markets.

There are three things you need to know about the SIP:

1) You can watch the SIP, you can't trade on the SIP
2) The SIP is faster than you but slower than other data (it ought to be faster)
3) It is sometimes used for "trade-through" protection, sometimes not

Lewis aptly describes the SIP as the consolidated picture of the market's best prices on every exchange. Since it must consolidate the best prices from eleven different exchanges, it will, by definition, always be slower than obtaining data directly from the exchange. For example, if you are at a meeting and you ask for a show of hands for and against a proposal, you'll observe that while you can quickly tell what any individual's vote is, it takes a while to count and consolidate the votes for a final tally.

So it is with the SIP: it is guaranteed to be slower than the markets' direct data feeds since it must consolidate all the market data from every source. Although Lewis tells us it may be as much as 25 milliseconds slower than direct exchange data feeds, the research that Lewis references three paragraphs later says it's less than 5 milliseconds difference – more than five times faster than Lewis' unsubstantiated estimate. If you're a human, either number is many times faster than your reaction time. If you're a computer, you may or may not want something a little faster. Unfortunately, the SIP's maintenance is funded by a consortium of the exchanges, and none of them are inclined to spend a cent more than necessary. Ideally, the SEC would prod them to invest in a real revamp of this aging technology.

What does one do with the SIP? Not that much. It's basically like the ticker on the bottom of the CNBC screen – it shows you useful information, but it says little about the price at which your trade will occur.

Trades occur on exchanges, not the SIP. Specifically, trades occur when exchanges match incoming orders against the limit orders resting at the exchange, each of which has a specific price. If you send a limit order to that exchange that matches one of these prices, you get that price, not whatever price the SIP displays. If you sent a market order to that exchange, the price you get is the "market" price of the orders already resting at the exchange, not the SIP. Trades occur at the market prices, not the prices shown on the SIP.

Imagine that the SIP says that the market for AAPL is 400.00 – 400.02 and I want to buy at the market offering price, which looks like $400.02. Unbeknownst to me, a new, better offer arrives at the exchange to sell at $400.01. Before the SIP is updated, I send my market order to purchase AAPL to that exchange. I get the new, better price of $400.01. I do not buy at the old, worse price of $400.02 still displayed on the SIP. Trades occur on markets, not the SIP. In effect, viewing the SIP is similar to listening to your friend recount the price of gas he saw on his drive home from work – it's useful information, but you can't ask your friend to sell you gas at the prices he relays. Nor can you go to the gas station and tell them you want the price that your friend Joe saw a few hours ago.

In truth, you probably don't ever see the current SIP prices anyway. Most retail brokers – the kind you and I use to invest – display prices that are delayed by fifteen minutes. If you pay your broker a little more, they will show you "realtime" data. This data is filtered through their systems, sent out to you over the Internet and then crunched by your web browser. By the time the data gets to you or me, it's seconds old. That's fine by me, since (a) it takes me at least ten seconds to enter my order, and (b) neither I, nor anyone else, trades with the SIP anyway.

So again, what does one do with the SIP?

It's basically a cheap way to show approximately what the current market is. It's great for CNBC or your favorite Internet finance site, and probably adequate for any retail investor who doesn't live next to an exchange and doesn't possess super-human reflex times.

Professional investors have the choice of viewing the SIP or using direct feeds from the exchanges. Those who trade occasionally may chose the SIP for reasons of cost. Anyone who trades frequently will likely chose direct feeds (either from the exchange or a third-party consolidator), since they provide "depth of book" information – that is, information on the second-best price, and the third-best price, etc. This "depth of book" is critical information for block traders like Katsuyama who need to gauge the potential price impact of their orders by seeing how many shares are available beyond the best price. (Yes, that's right – Katsuyama probably wasn't using the SIP either.)

The other use of the SIP is to ensure customers get the best price by enforcing the "trade-through" rule. When incoming orders match the price of limit orders resting at the exchange, the customer is not allowed to receive a worse price than the consolidated price on the SIP. For example, if a broker tries to buy AAPL shares for his customer on an exchange without much volume, the best offer on that exchange might be $400.50. If the SIP showed the national best offer to be $400.08, the broker's attempt to buy at $400.50 would be rejected by the exchange, since the customer is getting a worse price than the best price possible. The broker cannot "trade-through" the better price to stick his customer with a worse price. Instead, the broker must buy at $400.08, obtaining the best possible price for his customer.

Regulation NMS is responsible for giving us trade-through protection. It not only protects you from your broker making a mistake and sending your order to the wrong exchange, it even protects you if the prices changed while your order was being sent. In other words, if, in the time between when your broker chose an exchange and the time that his order arrived at that exchange, a better price became available elsewhere, the exchange will prevent the trade.

We'll spend more time on trade-through rules later, but for now know that it's a very important – though imperfect – protection for investors.

AAPL and the SIP: Not So Fast

"[T]he SIP might suggest to the ordinary investor in Apple Inc. that the stock was trading at 400-400.01. The investor would then give his broker his order to buy 1,000 shares at the market price, or $400.01. The infinitesimal period of time between the moment the order was submitted and the moment it was executed was gold to the traders with faster connections. How much gold depended on two variables: a) the gap in time between the public SIP and the private ones and b) how much Apple's stock price bounced around. The bigger the gap in time, the greater the chance that Apple's stock price would have moved; and the more likely that a fast trader could stick an investor with an old price. That's why volatility was so valuable to high-frequency traders: It created new prices for fast traders to see first and to exploit. It wouldn't matter if some people in the market had an early glimpse if the price of Apple's shares never moved.

Apple's stock moved a lot, of course. In a paper published in February 2013, a team of researchers at the University of California, Berkeley, showed that the SIP price of Apple stock and the price seen by traders with faster channels of market information differed 55,000 times in a single day. That meant that there were 55,000 times a day a high-frequency trader would exploit the SIP-generated ignorance of the wider market. Fifty-five thousand times a day, he might buy Apple shares at an outdated price, then turn around and sell them at the new, higher price, exploiting the ignorance of the slower-footed investor on either end of his trades."

Like Lewis' earlier examples of "latency tables," this example suffers from the same two problems: 1) it's impossible, and 2) if one attempted this strategy, one would lose a lot of money.

It's impossible to trade with the SIP. As mentioned above, trades occur when orders are matched at the same price. One doesn't trade "with the SIP". When Lewis opines that "a fast trader could stick an investor with an old price," this is simply impossible. When he doubles-down on this theory, his own phrasing belies the absurdity of the situation: "Fifty-five thousand times a day, [a high-frequency trader] might buy Apple shares at an outdated price." If the price is outdated, it means that the orders in the market no longer reflect that price – how can one buy at that price?

Let's dig into the second part of the example that Lewis sets up, but doesn't complete (perhaps because it's impossible to do so?):

> "Fifty-five thousand times a day, [a high-frequency trader] might buy Apple shares at an outdated price, then turn around and sell them at the new, higher price, exploiting the ignorance of the slower-footed investor on either end of his trades."

With Apple trading at 400.00 – 400.01, the SIP indicates one can buy Apple at $400.01. While the "slower-footed" investor is looking at the SIP data the actual market nudges up to 400.01 – 400.02. What happens if Lewis' imaginary high-frequency trader tries to buy shares at the outdated SIP price of $400.01? Nothing. The price of his buy order, $400.01, is lower than the new offer at $400.02, and it doesn't match it. No trade. Trades only occur when the prices of the orders match. It's impossible for him to buy the shares at an outdated price.

And therefore yet another scam described by Lewis is impossible.

Fixing Lewis' example. After reading Lewis' example, I spent a long time trying to figure out if there was some way to fix it to make it possible, let alone credible. There isn't, at least not in the public stock markets. However, it might be possible outside the public markets, in private dark pools. Interestingly, the research that Lewis cites, but presumably didn't read, provides one hypothetical example – but it requires six different pre-conditions to be possible. Specifically, it requires professional traders who (a) choose to trade in two separate dark pools, (b) use resting orders and not market orders, and (c) use an esoteric order type known as a mid-point peg. The purely speculative part is that the example would also require that (d) there exists a dark pool #1 that relies on the SIP to compute a mid-point peg but (e) there exists another dark pool #2 that does not rely on the SIP to compute a mid-point peg, and (f) there is some predator who knows precisely when both dark pools (which don't broadcast any market data) update these computations and precisely how many shares each has available in mid-point peg orders. Lewis' example contains none of these six qualifiers, which together narrow the possible scenarios to almost zero, if not actually zero. In doing so, he created something that sounded sinister, but is nearly impossible.

Why Apple? If you're curious why Lewis choose Apple ("AAPL") as his example, just read the research he is relying upon:

> "AAPL has three times more dislocations than the next highest security, Amazon.com, but the average size of these dislocations is only one basis point...The dislocations statistics suggest that the illustrative numbers for the costs of latency for AAPL in Section 5 do not directly generalize to other securities. Because AAPL is a very active high-priced

stock the percentage size of dislocations is much smaller, but dislocations occur much more often than in other securities."[40]

In other words, AAPL is an extreme outlier in three dimensions that matter for this example: (1) The high price means that the smallest twitch in value of the company moves the stock price by at least a penny (this is the opposite of the Sirius share price example previously), (2) it is a highly volatile technology company with more changes in company value than other traditional companies, and (3) it trades more shares daily than almost any other company. It was, of course, the most valuable company in the world when this experiment was conducted in the spring of 2012. In other words, it's pretty much impossible to extrapolate anything from the way Apple's stock behaves to the rest of the market – just as the researchers say.

Meeting with the SEC

In the spring of 2010, the SEC issued a broad call for comments and information on stock market structure and, specifically comments on high-frequency trading. Despite the concerns Katsuyama was apparently articulating on his Wall Street sales calls

---

[40] This quote is found in the actual published version of the paper, "How Slow Is the NBBO? A Comparison with Direct Exchange Feeds," Ding, Hanna, Hendershott, *The Financial Review*, May, 2014. The version that Lewis says was "published" in February 2013 by "a team of researchers at the University of California, Berkeley" was, in truth, merely uploaded to the website of Redline Systems, the company that sells the market data system used in the study (and benefits from showing how often its system is faster than the cheaper alternative, the SIP). The authors were not a "team" from Berkeley; while Hendershott teaches there, lead author Ding works at Wells Fargo Securities. Hanna's credentials are literally blotted out in the 2013 version, perhaps due to an apparent conflict of interest for the Director of Business Development at Redline Systems to be acknowledged as one of the paper's authors. He is simply listed without any credentials in the final version published in Financial Review.

at that time, he declined to submit any public comment to the SEC.[41] This is a shame, because the SEC did receive comments from many market participants – over two hundred that year – covering every topic that Katsuyama mentions in the book. These comments have played a large role in regulatory changes in the past four years, and it's baffling that he spurned the opportunity to be a part of it.

A year or two later, Katsuyama's bosses finally decide that if he is alleging rampant fraud in the stock market on his sales calls, he ought to mention this to the SEC. Interestingly, he doesn't propose to supply the SEC with data and evidence about the purported fraud – in fairness, *Flash Boys* supplies no such evidence to make its case either – but instead he wants to tell them about his product: "It was more about not wanting them to be embarrassed about not knowing about Thor than it was us thinking they were going to do something about it."

After Katsuyama describes his product to the SEC, he relates that the regulators debated whether or not Thor's technique of simultaneously hitting all the market-makers on all the different exchanges was fair to the market-makers.[42] Lewis doesn't really offer much on that debate, other than to imply that the SEC didn't act on Katsuyama's presentation (it's unclear what action they were asked to take, if any) because, "The SEC, like the public stock exchanges, had a kind of equity stake in the future revenues of high-frequency traders." As with the flash crash report, if the conclusion doesn't suit, Lewis attempts to discredit the people involved, instead of addressing the actual arguments.

---

[41] Only three years later, as *Flash Boys* neared publication, did RBC submit any public comment to the SEC on the topic. There is no mention, positive or negative, of high-frequency trading.

[42] Lewis eschews the phrase "market-makers," instead writing that an SEC staffer said *What you are doing is not fair to high-frequency traders.* Lewis avoids using quotation marks here, perhaps because this is his own, colorful paraphrasing. In my own discussions with SEC staff, they would typically use the more precise and accurate term "market-makers" in this context.

Later in the same chapter Lewis heaps praise on the very same people he just heaped scorn upon: "The people who worked in the SEC's Division of Trading and Markets were actually great—nothing like what the public imagined. They were smart and asked good questions and even spotted small mistakes in Gates's presentation." Not surprisingly, Lewis' praise comes after a second meeting where the staff took a position that he agreed with.

I'm glad that Lewis ultimately does recognize the people at Trading and Markets, even if his motivations are suspect. I've met with them many times, and found that they are very smart people who have a comprehensive picture of the market that nobody else does. Unlike the higher-profile departments of the SEC that investigate and enforce regulations, this select team focuses exclusively on writing the regulations.[43] Like the Supreme Court, they are reviled no matter how they decide a rule – somebody always feels disadvantaged. Also like the Supreme Court, they write extensive justifications for their choices where they present both sides of the argument and supply their rationale for choosing one over the other. I've disagreed with a fair number of their rule changes, particularly during the financial crisis, but I have to admit that they always had a plausible rationale that was backed by extensive data.

The debate Lewis describes at Katsuyama's meeting with the SEC is interesting for a number of reasons. For example, for the first time Lewis admits that high-frequency traders might have another business line outside of the (impossible) front-running scam he has concocted: they might be market-makers.

As market-makers, they take the risk of always being ready to buy or sell stock. As mentioned in the discussion of Chapter 2, market-makers will adjust their prices up or down based on risk, and based on supply and demand. If some trader using Thor bought up

---

[43] More directly, these guys had nothing to do with the Madoff debacle, Enron, etc.

all the shares on the NYSE, NASDAQ, and BATS, a market-maker on the Boston Stock Exchange would think that (a) this new surge in demand will push the price higher, and (b) my offer to sell at the current price is a big risk since the price is about to shoot higher. While this market-maker is pondering this, Thor hits them, too. For the idea of Thor was, of course, to jump all the market-makers on all the exchanges at the same time, before even the last ones could react to the new price. The fact that some might see this tactic as rather predatory may have been why RBC's upper management thought it might be a good idea to seek the SEC's blessing before widely publicizing Thor.

Was Thor predatory? From one perspective, the market-makers were professionals, and part of their job was to manage risk. Even if Thor increased their risk and stuck them with losses, they were professionals and this was the bargain they had struck.

The other perspective was that Thor was unfair because it effectively preyed on slower market-makers who didn't anticipate Katsuyama's blitzkrieg. Market-makers are an essential part of the markets – the markets simply can't function without them – and taking advantage of them raises some eyebrows. Thor was a way to push all the natural price impact of an order onto the market-makers: Thor took all their shares before they could react, and they were stuck with a losing position in the millisecond before the market adjusted to the new price caused by Thor's surge in demand. It was as if they were still offering an outdated price that didn't reflect the price impact of Thor's trades on all the other exchanges, and Thor took advantage of this. From this angle, the intent of Thor was to use latency to trick these market-makers into doing something they didn't want to do.

To me, this is a very interesting debate. Personally, I'd side with Katsuyama on this one and say that the market-makers agreed to take on risk and had to accept it. That said, I don't know that I would use Thor personally. The premise of using latency to trick market-makers into bearing the price impact that I caused isn't illegal, but it does seem to prey on a particular weakness of a particular (essential) class of market participant. Price impact can be managed in much better ways that don't involve smacking the market and exacerbating volatility.

The Argument for HFT: Spreads and Liquidity

"Back when human beings sat in the middle of the stock market, the spreads between the bids and offers of any given stock were a sixteenth of a percentage point. Now that computers did the job, the spread, at least in the more actively traded stocks, was typically a penny, or one-hundredth of 1 percent. That, said the supporters of high-frequency trading, was evidence that more HFT meant more liquidity."

If it seems like the last sentence doesn't logically follow from the previous sentence, it's because it doesn't. Lewis cleverly sets up the argument in favor of high-frequency trading as a nonsensical bogeyman, and then proceeds to muddy the waters even more, spending pages explaining why the word he just misused, "liquidity," doesn't really mean anything.

Let's return to the beginning. First, what is the significance of the spread between bids and offers? It's the amount that you typically pay to get into and out of an investment (using market orders). Imagine that you want to invest in ABC, which is bid at $10.00 and offered at $10.06. The difference between the bid and offer is six cents. This doesn't seem like much, right? Say you buy 100 shares at $10.06. You invested wisely, and the stock appreciates by 6%. Now the stock is bid at $10.60 and offered at $10.66. You sell your shares at 10.60. You made $0.54 cents per share – not the 6% return you expected, but actually a 5.4% return. Where did the money go?

That extra money vanished into "the spread." Ten percent of your return disappeared. Poof. This is why the spread is quite important: if it is big, you waste a lot of investment dollars. If you can shrink the spread, your investments earn a lot more.

So, how much has the spread shrunk? Lewis tells us that computerized trading has reduced spreads from a "sixteenth of a percentage point" to "one-hundredth of 1 percent." There are few better techniques to obscure an argument than to make the reader compare fractions. So, let us convert Lewis' fractions into decimal percentages: the spread dropped from 0.0625% to 0.0100%. Put another way, **Lewis tells us that the transaction costs to buy and sell your stock dropped six times lower after we moved to a computerized market.** That's a pretty powerful argument in favor of computerization. No wonder Lewis buried it under a pile of fractions, and then topped the grave with a non sequitur about liquidity.[44]

Lewis doesn't want to dwell on the possibility that high-frequency market-makers have made the trading costs of the bid-offer spread six times lower for investors. Instead, he quickly launches into a meaningless tangent to say that increased trading volume doesn't mean better markets. He capably proves this obvious point, and for the rest of the book never touches the argument about vastly reduced trading costs again. It's too bad, because this is quite important. Smaller spreads are a huge, huge, win for investors. Here's what Vanguard, the world's largest single mutual fund manager, wrote to the SEC on the topic:

> "While the data universally demonstrate a significant reduction in transaction costs over the last ten to fifteen years, the precise percentages vary (estimates have ranged from a reduction of 35% to more than 60%). Vanguard estimates are in this range, and we conservatively estimate

---

[44] Actually, Lewis' claim that spreads were a sixteenth of a percentage point when "human beings sat in the middle of the market" is hard to match to any data that I've seen. It's most likely that he is comparing the legal minimum price increment over time. By law, stocks traded in eighths of a dollar ($0.125) until 1997 and sixteenths of a dollar until 2001 ($0.0625). Actual spreads were *wider*, but they couldn't be any smaller.

that transaction costs have declined 50 bps, or 100 bps round trip. This reduction in transaction costs provides a substantial benefit to investors in the form of higher net returns. For example, if an average actively managed equity mutual fund with a 100% turnover ratio would currently provide an annual return of 9%, the same fund would have returned 8% per year without the reduction in transaction costs over the past decade. Today's investor with a 30 year time horizon would see a $10,000 investment in such a fund grow to approximately $132,000 in 30 years, compared to approximately $100,000 with the hypothetical return of 8% associated with the higher transaction costs. This roughly 25% decrease in the end value of the investment demonstrates the impact of reduced transaction costs on long-term investors. Thus, any analysis of "high frequency trading" must recognize the corresponding benefits that long-term investors have experienced through tighter spreads and increased liquidity."[45]

It's worth reading this a second time. The world's largest mutual fund manager writes that when you retire, your investment would be 25% smaller without the benefit of the decreased costs wrought by computerized trading. This is incredibly important.

Lewis does admit that, "spreads in the market had narrowed – that much was true." He dismisses the role of high-frequency trading in this improvement with the claim that the spread would have narrowed anyway "with the automation of the stock market." What does this mean? Exchanges, automated or not, don't make prices – market participants do. Presumably, then, Lewis means the automation of stock market participants caused trading costs to plummet. If he is arguing that market participants started using computers to automate trading and this resulted in narrower spreads, then he is right – and these automated, computerized

[45] See Letter from Gus Sauter, Managing Director and Chief Investment Officer, The Vanguard Group, to the Securities and Exchange Commission, dated April 21, 2010.

market-makers sound an awful lot like high-frequency traders. It's no coincidence that one of the original high-frequency trading firms was called Automated Trading Desk. So, yes, automation in the stock market has narrowed spreads. That's exactly what high-frequency market-makers do.

Lewis' final fallback position is that the narrower spreads today aren't really real, but are "an illusion." His complaint is the same as in Chapter 2: "the minute you went to buy or sell at the stated market price, the price moved." Clearly, this wasn't the experience of Vanguard. Apparently, this wasn't even the experience of Lewis' hero. On Bloomberg TV, Katsuyama explained that when he said that the prices he saw "weren't actually what I could buy or sell in the market," he actually could trade (and did trade) at those prices – what he meant was that he could not immediately execute his *entire large order* at the premium price he wanted.[46] This isn't sinister, this is supply and demand, economics 101. They could pay another penny or two to transact the remainder of their super-sized order, but they choose instead to try their luck outsmarting the market. Some folks, perhaps, are able to do so. Others, perhaps not so lucky, blame illusions.

Risk and High-Frequency Traders

> *"Right now, if you are in one of the big banks, the profit center is the trading desk, and you can generate a huge amount of bonuses by making some big bets; you will be rewarded on the upside. If you make a really bad bet, a lot of times you've already banked all your bonuses. You might end up leaving the shop, but in the meantime everybody else is left holding the bag."*
>
> *– President Barack Obama, July 2, 2014*

---

[46] See "Katsuyama, Narang, Lewis Debate Speed Trading," Bloomberg TV, April 2, 2014.

One of the strangest complaints in *Flash Boys* is that high-frequency traders don't take enough risk.

Today our economy is still clawing its way out of the destruction of the financial crisis of 2008. The entire financial industry took on massive amounts of risk betting on the housing market, using arcane financial alchemy to magnify wagers that nobody understood. We all know how that story ended. (Read Lewis' book *The Big Short* if you don't.)

It's a measure of how easily we forget that Lewis is complaining that some firms aren't losing money often enough. Specifically, Lewis bemoans the fact that two large electronic market-making firms rarely have a losing day, and therefore they must be cheating. Apparently, good, honest Wall Street firms demonstrate their integrity by frequently losing large sums of money.

It's absurd, but I feel that I am forced to argue it's O.K. for a firm to *not* blow up, especially market-making firms that don't subsist on the speculative trading that characterizes old Wall Street. There are a number of reasons that a market-maker can be consistently profitable, none of which are sinister. For example:

1) The Law of Large Numbers
2) Automation of Risk Controls
3) Simplicity
4) Smart People Not Paid to Take Excess Risk

The Law of Large Numbers. The law of large numbers is the fancy name probability theory gives to the well-known fact that the Yankees almost always have a winning season. Over the past 22 years, the Yankees have won 59% of the time – a little better than even. But even if you win just slightly more often than you lose, if you do this consistently for all 162 games in the season, you are likely to come out ahead. This is why the Yankees have had only one losing season in the past 22 years.

The same principle applies to trading. If a firm has a 52.5% chance of making a penny on a trade and a 47.5% chance of losing a penny, and it makes five thousand trades a day it will only have one losing day every eight years.[47] It's not mysterious, it's basic statistics. Lewis' claim that the only explanation for a multi-year winning streak is a criminal one – "This sort of performance is possible only if you have a huge informational advantage" – is only shocking because it shows an utter disregard for elementary analysis in his rush to level accusations.

The real question, then, is why do financial firms lose money at all if they only need to win slightly more often than they lose?

In many cases, the answer is the mixture of greed and hope that lies at the heart of financial speculation. A traditional trader with a profitable trade wants a little more, and holds on until the market turns against him. A trader with a losing trade thinks he can cut his losses if he just waits a little longer, and the market continues to go against him. Computers don't have hope. A market-making algorithm is programmed to buy and sell at the current market prices, and earn one penny more often than it loses one. Human traders want to hit home runs and take home huge bonuses. Computers are programmed to hit singles and increase the odds of giving the team a win.[48]

Automation. The automation of risk controls – now mandated for all broker-dealers by the SEC – plays a factor as well. Years ago, if

---

[47] See http://mcarreira.typepad.com/mc_notes/2014/03/a-simple-model-for-the-pl-of-a-market-maker-how-many-losing-days-in-a-year.html for a simple mathematical model of how a small win percentage turns into many winning days.

[48] The old Wall Street approach of hope and greed permeates all of Lewis' trading examples: every time a trader has a position, Lewis tells us that the trader could just wait a while for the market to go his way; there is never a thought that the market might turn against him. This is an incredibly naive way to go bankrupt, fast.

there was any risk management at all on trading desks, it was a gut feeling based on a weekly check of trading positions. Today's trading algorithms evaluate the risk of a position *before* the trade is made, *while* the trade is executing, *and* every millisecond thereafter. Many firms have multiple redundant systems checking risk at all times. The "traders" are actually risk managers, continually responding to mini alarms that signal the slightest anomaly.

There are no hidden positions – like the ones that caused the $6 billion "London Whale" loss for JPMorgan – because all the trades automatically flow into these risk management systems, instantly double-checked against redundant data feeds from the exchanges. Rogue traders have no room to hide risky positions. Unlike banks trading opaque financial instruments that only a few insiders understand, high-frequency firms transact in liquid, well-understood exchange-traded securities.

Simplicity. Market-makers trade what they understand. This seems simple, and it is. Banks, hedge funds, and even pension funds trade financial assets that are harder to understand, and harder to price properly when accounting for risk. The complexity in evaluating these assets is why the reward is sometimes so great – Goldman Sachs may make millions on a single trade, where a market-maker is looking at a handful of pennies. On the other hand, the complexity is a two-edged sword that may result in a loss of millions (or billions) for a big bank.

These are almost two completely distinct business models, say, selling greeting cards versus buying and selling modern art. One business brings consistent profits from a high volume of sales, most of which are profitable. The other may bring far greater profits or big losses. Ten years ago hedge fund titan Steven A. Cohen bought a piece by modern art phenom Damien Hirst for $8 to $12 million. Was this piece, a tiger shark embalmed in formaldehyde, worth that much? Far more? Far less? Who knows? The only guarantee is that the returns of such an investment will not be consistent or predictable. The guy selling greeting cards, though, is likely to consistently make a small profit. The profits won't pay for a house in the Hamptons, but he's guaranteed a steady paycheck. It's reliable and simple.

The simplicity of a market-maker's portfolio not only makes it easy to monitor known current risks, but also to respond quickly as new risks emerge. For example, the week that Lehman Brothers declared bankruptcy in 2008, almost all of Wall Street ground to a halt. At the banks, armies of traders and lawyers combed through mountains of trade records and financial contracts in a vain attempt to determine their exposure to Lehman Brothers. Many stopped even answering the phone. For electronic market-makers, though, it was business as usual. There were no CDSes, CMBSes, ABSes, or other obscure entanglements to ponder. Without such distractions, they could continue to focus on their core business as they navigated through very difficult times. Risk management of a simpler business was, well, simpler.

People. As Lewis notes, the people working at high-frequency firms are not the chest-thumping alpha males he saw on trading floors more than twenty years ago. In general, they are extremely intelligent, highly analytical, and methodical. These are the people designing the risk management systems, and they are exactly the people one would want managing risk in our financial system – particularly given how well the other character-type has worked out.

Wall Street typically rewards traders bonuses based on their profit, with little penalty for losses. This perverse incentive system encourages excess risk taking (again, read *The Big Short*). At many high-frequency trading firms, employees are compensated as much for their risk management as for the profit they help generate, encouraging prudence.

Average compensation is actually well below Wall Street standards – Katsuyama's salary of $2 million is higher than any *total* employee compensation package I have ever offered a high-frequency trader. Obviously his "opening bid" of $3 million a year was higher too. A brief conversation with a compensation consultant about high-frequency norms, or perhaps a chat with an employee of a high-frequency firm, would have set Lewis straight on this score.[49] Undoubtedly, employees are well compensated but they could make much more money at Goldman Sachs, or even RBC, they just choose not to work in a big bank. They prefer flip-flops to wingtips, and, in my experience, don't like to have a chest-thumping alpha male yelling at them. At my former firm, prospective employees weighed offers from other flip-flop friendly companies like Facebook, Google, and other tech companies – and sometimes chose them due to *better* compensation packages.

Lewis tackles the question of personnel later in this chapter, again throwing us for a loop. He doesn't breathe a sigh of relief that cooler and smarter heads are now prevailing in trading. He doesn't speculate on whether or not the recent influx of smart engineers into finance is part of the reason that trading costs have declined so significantly for the Vanguards of the world. Instead, he unleashes a bizarre, condescending soliloquy: why don't these scientists and engineers go back to where they belong, in the labs, instead of competing with the old guard for well-paid jobs on Wall Street?

His disdain for high-frequency traders is so great (they "had no idea of the meaning of their own lives") and he rushes to pass judgment so quickly that he doesn't even bother to get the facts right about their backgrounds. For example, the phrase "the French particle physicist from FERMAT lab" caught my eye immediately. There are no particle physicists at "FERMAT lab," but there are many

---

[49] The lone example from which Lewis extrapolates, Misha Malyshev, was a partner at a hedge fund called Citadel, and founded their electronic options trading fund. To infer industry-wide compensation based on this individual is absurd – akin to inferring computer programmer salaries based on Bill Gates' compensation.

at Fermi Lab. Perhaps it's too much to ask, but if you're going to judge people based on a single fact about their lives, at least it ought to be accurate. Better still, why don't you get to know the person before passing judgment at all? Maybe his or her story will enlighten you.

As it turns out, I actually do know this person. Like many other Americans (yes, he's American but his LinkedIn profile notes that he speaks French), at some point many PhDs want a career change. Not only may they find something else more intellectually stimulating, but the challenge of supporting a family on a salary that is less than 5% of Katsuyama's salary starts to get old.[50] After various jobs in the technology industry, he landed in finance. He chose not to work on Wall Street due to its culture. Instead, he applied his extraordinary intellect to the business of electronic market-making, and in doing so significantly reduced trading costs in the stock market, benefiting all of us who invest in it. While Lewis condemns the life choices of a man he never met, I'd say it's remarkable that somebody found a job where he can benefit society as a whole, tackle intellectual challenges, and support his family.

Before casting aspersions on a lot of good people, I wish Lewis had pondered the implications if he were wrong about his theory. What if the broad industry consensus, that high-frequency trading has benefited everyone who invests in the markets, is right? What if, instead of perpetrating a vast conspiracy of thievery, these people instead had dramatically reduced trading costs and thus significantly increased the size of our retirement accounts? What if they had applied their considerable smarts to squeezing out inefficiencies in the markets, thereby rebating hundreds of millions of dollars to investors every day?

---

[50] The annual salary for many physics PhDs is less than annual grad school tuition. It's a shame that we're wasting time debating whether it's acceptable for a PhD to pursue a business career instead of talking about the underlying problem of how we underfund our sciences.

It would make a good story, perhaps even more entertaining than *Flash Boys*. It was, and is, a true Wall Street revolt: the geeks versus the Gordon Geckos, computer nerds who overthrew the skimming specialists of yesteryear and made investing cheaper for everyone. Best of all, this story is true.

Managing risk. Lastly, Lewis' complaint that high-frequency traders bear no risk because high-frequency traders "go home flat every night" and "don't take positions" is false. Large traders must file Form 13F reports with the SEC on a quarterly basis, detailing their largest positions. You, Michael Lewis, or anyone for that matter can Google "Form 13F" for your favorite trading firm and see its largest positions. The most recent report available for Getco / KCG Holdings shows a portfolio of at least $6.4 billion.[51] You'll get similar results for any number of high-frequency trading firms. Most people would say that owning a few billion dollars worth of stock is a pretty large position.

Even if the high-frequency traders did go home flat, it wouldn't mean that they bear no risk. Ask any day trader out there whether or not he has lost money. The answer is of course yes. The longer you hold a stock, the more risk you bear. But there is no period of time, however miniscule, where you can hold stock without any risk. Period. It's incredibly naive to imply otherwise.

Fortunately, positions or not, most high-frequency traders seem to manage the risk pretty well. Unlike much of Wall Street, they aren't speculators taking a joy ride with their investors' money. I'm still not sure why that bothers Lewis.

---

[51] See Form 13F filing of KCG Holdings Inc (formerly Knight Capital and Getco) as of June 30, 2014.

Fun With Numbers (again): Lewis Argues With Himself About Profits

To measure the cost to the economy of high-frequency trading "you needed to know how much money [these firms] made. That was not possible," Lewis laments. "The new intermediaries were too good at keeping their profits secret."

Lewis is clearly frustrated that he cannot figure out the profits of the high-frequency trading industry. This is curious since these estimates are not hard to find, if one has access to the Internet. Larry Tabb – whose research Lewis quotes in Chapter 1 on the trading value of the Spread Networks fiber-optic line – estimates high-frequency trading in U.S. stocks will generate $1.3 billion in total revenue in 2014, down from a peak of $7.3 billion in 2009.[52] Rosenblatt Securities estimates annual profits to be about $1 billion in 2013, down from a peak of $5 billion in 2009.[53] If one dares to go one click beyond a Google search for "high-frequency profits" even more data is available. It's not hard to find, and it's certainly not a secret.

For example, Getco, a firm mentioned seven times by Lewis and likely the largest high-frequency firm, is a public company. Like any other public company, it submits quarterly financial reports to the SEC, which are published online. These reports contain detailed data on profits, revenues, expenses, and everything else under the sun. Anyone can download them, for free.

Perhaps the problem then isn't that Lewis couldn't find the data, but rather that the data he found didn't square with his conspiracy.

---

[52] See "Wall Street Market Structure Expert, TABB Group Research Firm Founder Larry Tabb Responds to CBS 60 Minutes Interview with Flash Boys Author," Reuters, April 1, 2014.

[53] See "Dark markets may be more harmful than high-frequency trading", John McCrank, Reuters, April 6, 2014.

For example, in Chapter 2, Lewis makes an estimate of what he deems to be the cost of high-frequency trading to the markets. It's allegedly $40 billion per year in front-running alone, as measured by a single trade by Thor.[54] In Chapter 6, he tells us that, "Slow market arbitrage...generated more billions of dollars a year than the other strategies combined." Putting this together, these two "strategies" would then total at least $80 billion a year – more than fifty times higher than the consensus of industry analysts.

Oddly, this number doesn't even square with the estimate Lewis squeezes between these two in Chapter 5: "financial intermediaries" collecting "somewhere between $10 billion and $22 billion a year, depending on whose estimates you wanted to believe." While we aren't told exactly who Lewis considers to be financial intermediaries, he does tell us that Goldman Sachs in this category, leading one to wonder, as Lewis says, what to believe.[55]

Regardless, even if Lewis had used the industry experts' estimates of $1 – 1.5 billion, it's still a lot of money. But using those real numbers would have led to the inevitable comparisons: RBC alone made half a billion dollars trading equities last year, Goldman made $2.6 billion, JPM made $4.8 billion.[56] The hedge fund heroes of his previous book, *The Big Short*, made much more than that shorting the U.S. housing market (John Paulson's *personal* take was $4 billion). Goldman Sachs pays more in bonuses every year than the entire high-frequency trading industry has made in the past three years.

---

[54] His estimate is "more than $160 million a day." With 250 trading days in the year, this comes to $40 billion annually.

[55] Katsuyama, who sat between investors and the markets, is of course an intermediary as well. Subtracting out Katsuyama and Goldman (who apparently are good guy intermediaries), we wind up with a number much lower than any of Lewis' other estimates.

[56] See "Michael Lewis Doesn't Like High-Frequency Traders," Matt Levine, BloombergView, March 31, 2014.

The problem with the real numbers for Lewis, then, is that they don't make high-frequency traders look like villains. They don't make them look like the guys "making perhaps more money than people have ever made on Wall Street." The real numbers make high-frequency traders look like, well, an entire industry that, when combined, makes only slightly more than Chipotle Mexican Grill.

Volatility – Incorrect Data Paired With Incorrect Analysis

"Scalpers Inc. was incentivized, for instance, to make the market as volatile as possible. The value of its ability to buy Microsoft from you at $30 a share and to hold the shares for a few microseconds – knowing that, even if the Microsoft share price began to fall, it could turn around and sell the shares at $30.01 – was determined by how likely it was that Microsoft's share price, in those magical microseconds, would rise in price."

Lewis faces a dilemma: how can you argue that volatility – the *unpredictability* of a stock's price – somehow benefits high-frequency traders, whom he has been arguing make all their money by *predicting* market moves? It seems that unpredictability would ruin whatever scam they have going. It's a very difficult argument to make, even more so given the principle of "adverse selection." Adverse selection is the fancy economic term that means that a market-maker who sticks his neck out is the first one to get stuck with a losing position when the market drops. The more volatile the markets, the more likely he gets stuck with losing positions.

Lewis' own volatility example above illustrates this: the market-maker bids to buy Microsoft at $30.00, you sell shares to him at that price, and the market begins to fall. It's obvious that if the market begins to fall, the market-maker's purchase of shares at the pre-fall price is a losing trade. Yet Lewis waves his hand and says it's not a problem since the market-maker apparently knows that "it could turn around and sell the shares at $30.01." While creative, this is completely false. The old price of $30.01 is gone. It's the *old* price. The market is now falling. The market-maker has to sell at the current, lower price. Just like everyone else, he loses money too when the market turns against him. Furthermore, if he wants to sell his shares immediately (because the market is falling), he has to sell at the current bid price, just like you.

If you think about it, Lewis is arguing that a market-maker wins, no matter which direction the market goes. Common sense says otherwise, and common sense is right. The market turns against market-makers just as often as it does everyone else – more so, in fact, because their resting orders put them on the wrong side of the trade when the market starts to move. If the market starts to fall, everyone sells to their resting bids and they have a losing long position. If the market starts to rise, everyone buys from their offers, and they have a losing short position.

Regardless, Lewis tries quite hard to claim that the markets are now much more volatile, and the only reason must be volatility-loving high-frequency traders. When Lewis tells us "the price volatility within each trading day in the U.S. stock market between 2010 and 2013 was nearly 40 percent higher than the volatility between 2004 and 2006," it's not clear what data source he is using. But it is clear that these are cherry-picked statistics: Why 2004 to 2006? Why not include 2003? And why compare to 2010, 2011, and 2012, with the European debt crisis threatening to blow apart Europe in a way that the U.S. housing crisis couldn't?[57]

---

[57] Lewis writes that "the financial crisis abated and the drama remained. There was no good explanation for this..." and proceeds to tell us that the only good explanation is that his front-running conspiracy caused the "drama." I think that the Greek, Portugal, Ireland, and Spain debt crises, along with the potential dissolution of the European Union, would qualify as good explanations of market volatility at that time. Lewis was well aware of this explanation: he penned an article about the Ireland debt crisis in Vanity Fair's March 2011 issue.

The answer is that the data fits his argument best when you slice it this way. The period from 2004 to 2006 comprises the quietest years on record – there were absolutely zero days where the market dropped by 2% or more, and only two days in those three years where the market rose by 2%. For contrast, in 2003 alone the market had 15 days where it rose or fell more than 2%. In 2002, there were more than 50 such days. So it's no surprise that Lewis excluded 2002 and 2003 from his "quiet" years.

In case you are wondering, market swings of 2% or more happened a whopping total of three days in 2013. I don't claim that the relative quiet of 2013 compared to 2003 proves that high-frequency trading has eliminated volatility. It simply means that 2013 was a relatively quiet year for the markets. This year is even quieter. As noted in a recent issue of the Economist, "volatility has collapsed to near-historic lows."[58]

Contrary to what Lewis wants us to think, market volatility is not created by three Russian programmers in New Jersey with a fiberoptic network. Market volatility is caused by geopolitical events and economic catastrophes: a revolution in Egypt; the US government threatening to default on its debt; the European Union falling apart; or the financial system imploding in 2008.

Scalpers Inc – Skip Interviews and Investigation, Use Imagination

Lewis' construction of the "Scalpers Inc" straw man says a lot about his book. In lieu of providing an interview with an actual trader at a real high-frequency firm, Lewis founds his own fictitious firm, called "Scalpers Inc." Freed from the constraints of reporting on companies that actually exist, he can imagine all sorts of bad things, speculating that "The bosses at Scalpers Inc would..." and "an earnest employee of Scalpers Inc would..."

---

[58] See "The Volatility Crash," The Economist, May 22, 2014.

Through this imagined vehicle, Lewis tells us things like high-frequency traders would look for ways to slow down the public's information: "The more time Scalpers could sit with some investor's stock market order, the greater the change that the price might move in the interim." But even after constructing a straw man out of whole cloth, he gets tripped up by not understanding the markets. If an investor submits a market order, it is executed immediately: it doesn't *sit* with anyone, for any period of time. In fact, market participants don't even see the order, they just see that a trade occurred after the fact. Conversely, if the investor submits a limit order with a particular price, they are guaranteed to receive that price or better. In either case, Lewis is dead wrong. Perhaps it would have been better to interview a real trader instead of imagining one?

Covering Losses – Proof of...Covering Losses

> *"I have no scientific evidence," said Brad. "This is purely a theory. But with Thor the HFT firms are trying to cover their losses. I'm short when I don't want to be, so I need to buy to cover, quickly."*

As discussed earlier, when Thor smacks all the market-makers simultaneously, they likely do scramble to cover their losses. This is what the SEC told Katsuyama months earlier: you've stuck all the market-makers with a losing position. Blindsided, they didn't have a chance to adjust to the new risk created by a huge order overwhelming the market. With the momentary spike in volatility due to Thor sweeping all the inventory of all the markets (the irony of the increase in volatility caused by Thor should not be lost) the market-makers panic, and immediately seek to cover their losses as soon as possible.

The strange thing is that Katsuyama and Lewis have finally come around to the same position that the junior SEC staffer figured out in a matter of minutes. But Katsuyama and Lewis can't let go of the inexplicable idea that somehow this pedestrian explanation also suggests a front-running conspiracy.

Their theory says more about them than anything else. They hypothesize that with "a winning position" one would have "the reckless abandon of gamblers playing with house money." This perfectly sums up the "old world" view of the equity trading desks at big banks like RBC, and it is the opposite of the computer-driven risk models employed today. Computers are not known for binges of reckless abandon. Humans sometimes are. And Wall Street traders, even more so.

Recall that equity desks at big banks like RBC would do client trades for a premium – in the book's first example, Katsuyama charges a client five cents per share to execute a trade. This is a "winning position," a built-in profit far greater than the fractions of pennies that Katsuyama alleges the high-frequency traders ever have. I can't speak for Katsuyama, but many big-bank equity traders take such opportunities to gamble with "house money." They figure that if the stock goes up, they take the profit (and pad their bonus), and if it goes down, they have a cushion of five cents before they have to report a loss to their bosses.

That is old Wall Street.

But economists and risk managers would beg to differ. They would say that your decisions about the future should only be based on your expectations about the future, not your past performance. The fact that you locked in a profit of five cents a minute ago doesn't say anything about your ability to make another penny trading in the next minute. If you now lose another four cents, you lost another four cents – you can't say that you "still made" one cent on the trade. Remarkably, old Wall Street still thinks this way, probably because at the end of the day the trader often reports the net profit of his trading *and* the customer's subsidy of his trading – so a four cent loss trading is cushioned by the customer's five cents, and the trader reports a net profit of one cent.

Economically, it's absurd. It's as if a baseball team signed an aging slugger who strikes out at every at bat, but then justifies it by saying he's still way ahead on his lifetime batting average. For some reason, Katsuyama and Lewis cling to this outdated and incorrect view of risk management, and make a leap of intuition to apply this illogic to others.

In the end, though, Brad is correct about one thing: Thor can cause market-making high-frequency traders to cover their losses. Why that implicates a vast conspiracy of front-running is beyond me.

The Market Behaves Expectedly: The Case of Dark Pools and Chipotle

A dark pool is an off-exchange venue for trading stocks, officially known as Alternative Trading System ("ATS"). Dark pools differ from exchanges in three major ways:

1) They are "dark". Unlike exchanges, dark pools do not disseminate market data –there is no data feed that tells a participant what prices or quantities are available on a dark pool in any given stock. On the other hand, dark pools do rely on public market data: trades in a dark pool can only occur if the execution price would match (or improve) the best prices displayed in the public markets.

2) They are very lightly regulated. There is little oversight of the rules under which dark pools operate, and almost no monitoring of their day-to-day operations. In contrast, exchanges are very highly regulated. Every rule and change they make must be approved by the SEC. Their day-to-day operations are monitored by the SEC, and, since all market data and trades are broadcast to the general public, the public also monitors everything that occurs.

3) They are opt-in, sort of. If an exchange has the sole best price in the stock one wants to trade, one is obligated to trade on that

exchange. In contrast, one is never required to trade on a dark pool. Brokers and professional traders must actively choose to connect to and trade on a dark pool. Unfortunately, retail investors aren't offered a choice. Their broker may send their orders to another broker ("payment for order flow," which we'll cover in Chapter 6), to a dark pool, or to a public exchange.

The main argument in favor of dark pools has been that being "dark" allows a trader with a very large order the ability to hide his intentions from the general market and hopefully mitigate the "price impact" of his trade (at least until he is done). Had Katsuyama traded his millions of shares in Solectron and AMD in a dark pool, the rationale goes, he might have completed the trade in one fell swoop, capturing the current market price before the market could react to the new change in supply and demand.

In practice, large dark pool orders are the exception, not the norm. The SEC performed an analysis of every order placed on a dark pool (ATS) in a given week in May 2012.[59] The SEC's Gregg Berman summarized one of the findings thusly:

> "In the week examined, about 28% of all market-wide volume was executed off-exchange. About 40% of that 28% was conducted on an ATS. That translates into 11% total market volume. And do you know what average order size was? Across all ATS, the average order size was only 374 shares. More so, over 60% of all orders entering into an ATS during the review period were for exactly 100 shares. Note that I am not referring to the size of trades *filled* on an ATS, but rather the size of orders *sent* to ATS.

---

[59] See Laura Tuttle, "Alternative Trading Systems: Description of ATS Trading in National Market System Stocks," SEC Division of Economic and Risk Analysis Memorandum, October 2013 (revised March 2014). Available at: http://www.sec.gov/marketstructure/research/alternative-trading-systems-march-2014.pdf

This data suggests that the buy-side uses the same algorithms in dark pools that they use on lit exchanges to slice up large orders into much smaller pieces to trade at the NBBO. And that gives me some pause, because it means there must be something more to the use of these algos than simply stating they are a necessary defense against the way quotes and trades are done on an exchange. Is trading in small size at the NBBO the only option, even in a dark pool?"[60]

In other words, few dark pools are being used to trade large blocks of stock.[61] If this is the case, what is the real reason dark pools exist?

One answer is exclusivity. Most dark pools are little side conversations in the markets, where a certain group of individuals can meet to transact. In a way, it's a throwback to the old Wall Street model of the prior century where many trades occurred not on the floor of the stock exchange, but "upstairs," privately negotiated between big bank brokers. Today, the *hoi polloi* is not on the floor of the exchange, but rather in the electronic matching engines of the exchange. To avoid them, Wall Street brokers choose to trade in a dark pool.

However, as Lewis tells us, the drawbacks are many: opaque rules, if any; little to no oversight on an ongoing basis by the regulators; additional software and network technology required to connect. The biggest drawback of all is that they are "dark" – there is no market data available to market participants about what the current prices and orders are. So when Lewis' next character, Rich Gates, wants "a test to see if there was anything in this new stock market to fear," he kicks aside the buyer-beware signs on the

---

[60] See Gregg Berman, "What Drives the Complexity and Speed of our Markets?" North American Trading Architecture Summit, April 15, 2014. See: http://www.sec.gov/News/Speech/Detail/Speech/1370541505819

[61] A small number of ATSs – five by the SEC's count – do cater to large orders.

entrance and plunges into a dark pool. If there is one place to fear, this is it. Gates gets what he signed up for, although Lewis, never satisfied, tweaks the example into impossibility again.

To start, Lewis tells us that Gates uses a "mid-point peg" order, which is an order type available only to professionals that rests in the market without any firm price. The desired price is the "mid-point," or middle, of the current market. Whenever the market changes, the order's price changes too. Like a market order, one doesn't know what price one is agreeing to; like a limit order, there is a risk that the order will never match another order, and therefore never actually execute. It's a strange mix that combines the worst of limit orders and market orders, and maximizes uncertainty. These drawbacks are probably why your broker doesn't give you the choice to place a "mid-point peg" order – in most cases you'd be quite unhappy with the result.

If Gates were seeking something to fear, then this is it: using an order type that guarantees neither price nor execution in a dark pool with few rules, no police, and zero visibility.

With the public markets apparently displaying 100.00 – 100.10, Gates places a mid-point peg order to buy Chipotle shares, expecting that, if he trades in the dark pool, he will get the price of $100.05. He next places a second order on a public exchange to sell Chipotle shares at $100.01. Lewis then inexplicably claims that, "He should have been able to buy from himself the shares he was selling at $100.01. But that's not what happened." Of course that's not what happened: he placed orders on completely different markets. He's trying to sell his car on eBay and offering to buy the same make and model of car on Craigslist. He's transacting on two separate marketplaces. Making it even worse, one of the marketplaces has a rule not to reveal that he is trying to transact there.

What actually happens is this: his order to buy shares executes at $100.05, the price he expected, and his order to sell executed at $100.01, the price he expected. The real issue isn't the prices he received – which are exactly what he asked for – but rather how the information about his order in a "dark" pool was known to somebody. That is troubling, and worth probing.

Dark pools don't disseminate market data to any of their clients, high-frequency or otherwise. But, as Lewis points out, clients didn't know "whether the Wall Street bank [running the dark pool] allowed its own proprietary traders to know of the big buy order." This is absolutely true. Some dark pool operators make no guarantees about their own trading in the dark pool. For those that promise that their bank's proprietary traders have no special advantages, it's still blind faith: unlike the public markets, there are few police on this beat. For this reason, many high-frequency traders choose *not* to trade in dark pools – they are afraid that the banks' traders will rip *them* off in the dark.

Still, some high-frequency traders do trade in dark pools. Lewis comes tantalizingly close to the real reason, but then veers off course again, lured by the siren song of his front-running conspiracy. The main answer is that banks send their customer orders through the dark pools, and customer orders are less likely to stick it to the market-makers, the way Thor stuck it to them. The technical term for this is "non-directional order flow." This means that most customers are selling due to personal reasons, not because the market is falling that instant. Professional traders, on the other hand, tend to sell when the market is dropping and buy when the market is rising. If you are a market-maker, customer orders are much less risky to handle. In some cases, that reduction of risk may offset the risks of trading in a dark pool, luring some market-makers into the pool.

Lewis overlooks this well-known explanation, and instead falls back on his front-running conspiracy to explain everything. He offers two arguments. First, he tells us that a customer's dark pool order is "especially predictable: Each Wall Street bank had its own detectable pattern for handling orders." While we debunked the pattern sniffing idea in the last chapter, here it's even more absurd: he is talking about a dark pool, and a single one at that. What good would his "latency tables" do when there is a single market? How does one see a "tell" from a broker's router when there is no market data? Of course, this is impossible. It doesn't matter how predictable it might be if you can't see it. Further, customer orders are small, and are almost always executed in a single transaction. If a predator could infer a "detectable pattern" from that single transaction (which is impossible – it's a single data point) it would be rather useless, since the order has already been completely executed.

His second argument is that a dark pool order is "slow, because of the time it was forced to spend inside the dark pool before accessing the wider market." This simply doesn't make sense. There is no bizarre order type that I know of that is held hostage in a dark pool for some period of time before being released to other markets. If there were, why would anyone choose that? Lewis is again forced to conjure up the impossible in order to make his argument.

Notably, Lewis abandons these inane arguments in his next example: there is no "detectable pattern," nor is there any order held hostage. Instead, he submits a new theory: "Any decent high-frequency trader who had paid for a special connection to the pool would ping the pool with tiny buy and sell orders in every listed stock, searching for activity. Once they'd discovered the buyer of Microsoft, they'd simply wait..."

Of course, if, as Lewis speculates, every "decent high-frequency trader" were pinging every dark pool in this way, one's order would execute pretty quickly as they chipped away at it.[62] That order for Chipotle would have been executed immediately, even if it were a large order – it would only take ten of these firms pinging to fill a 1,000 share order within milliseconds. But in the example he gave, it didn't happen. At all. There simply was no pinging.

---

[62] As an aside, in this scenario the dark pool would be barraged with buy and sell orders in more than 7,000 stocks every few milliseconds, multiplied by however many "decent high-frequency traders" were connected. This doesn't happen.

That aside, Lewis again avoids the obvious question of how all these predators would know the size of his hypothetical order to buy 100,000 shares of Microsoft, based on an execution of a single 100 share order. It's simply impossible. There may be 99,900 shares of Microsoft still in the dark pool, there may be zero. The only party that knows for sure is the one who submitted the order. The only other party that might know is the one that operates the dark pool.

Which brings us, full circle, back to where we started with dark pools. The Chipotle example didn't rely on high-frequency pinging, "detectable patterns," or orders held hostage. It did involve sending an order to Goldman Sachs' dark pool without any assurances about whether or not Goldman's proprietary trading group would have special access to the order. Rich Gates decided to see if there was anything to fear when he set up an arbitrage situation and dropped it into the lap of Goldman Sachs. Based on what Lewis wrote, it sounds like he found out.

Broker-dealers are High-Frequency Traders – or Anything Else

It's not critical to the book, but it's yet another demonstration of its ridiculous leaps that Lewis assumes that a trading venue – Credit Suisse's Crossfinder in this case – caters to high-frequency traders because it says that its clients are broker-dealers:

> "All the large high-frequency firms, Schwall knew, were "broker-dealers." They had to be, to gain the special access they had to the public stock exchanges. So Mathisson had not ruled out dealing with them..."

Almost every firm on Wall Street, save for hedge funds (which largely escape any regulation), is registered as a broker-dealer. RBC is a broker-dealer. So is your stock broker, online or not. By law, any firm that trades directly on an exchange must be a broker-dealer. In fact, the only firms allowed on Katsuyama's dark pool are those that are – you guessed it – registered broker-dealers. (Incidentally, Katsuyama's dark pool, IEX, is also a broker-dealer.)

None of this is in order to procure special access. Rather, this is a result of the Securities Act of 1934, which requires companies that trade securities to be regulated by the government. A firm that is not a broker-dealer – such as a hedge fund – has minimal regulation at best. A broker-dealer must abide by rules that, among other things, govern trading activities, risk management, accounting, and the amount of capital reserved to pay for any trading losses. Broker-dealers are subject to periodic audits, and the SEC can drop in *at any time* if they have the slightest suspicion about the broker-dealer's activities (and they do drop in). It's a good thing.

Personally, I'd be more worried about the hedge funds that ultimately fund Katsuyama's dark pool, who have virtually no regulator oversight. What do Scott Rothstein, Arthur Nadel, and Bernie Madoff have in common? Serving as hedge fund managers, and serving time in jail.

CHAPTER 5:

SERGEY ALEYNIKOV

There's not too much to add to this chapter, as (a) it mostly focuses on a single individual, and (b) it's largely a reprint of Lewis' September 2013 article, which benefitted from Vanity Fair's fact-checking team.

Goldman overreacted. They wanted to send a message to programmers everywhere, and they did: steal code, go to prison. It's pretty harsh, but, I suppose, effective.

In his race to skewer Goldman, though, Lewis tries a little too hard to paint Aleynikov as an angel, and in the process again demonstrates a tendency to avoid critical evaluation of the facts.

For example, Lewis tells us that after Aleynikov copies Goldman's source code to a third party location for later retrieval:

> "...then he did what he had always done since he'd first started programming computers: He deleted his bash history – the commands he had typed into his own Goldman computer keyboard. To access the computer, he was required to type his password. If he didn't delete his bash history, his password would be there to see, for anyone who had access to the system."

From a technical perspective, this is rife with errors. First, one's "bash history" is not visible to anyone who has access to a system. It is only visible to the system's administrators. The system's administrators can already see any file on the system, and they don't need Sergey's password to do so. Further, a user's login password is never stored in the bash history anyway.

The only password that one might find in the bash history would be one that Aleynikov used to connect to the third-party server to which he sent Goldman's source code.[63] Even in that case, it's quite unusual for anyone to specify a password on the command line – in fact, it's against all security best practices. Many applications don't even permit it. They require the user to type the password in after running the command.

All in all, erasing the history of what he did sounds pretty fishy. Imagine a 7-Eleven manager, suspected of stealing from the store's safe, who wiped the closed-circuit video tapes of the store that night. His explanation: he always wiped the video tapes when he took cash from the register to put into the safe, because he didn't want somebody to be able to see the safe's combination by looking at the video. It's remotely possible that he had only the purest intentions, and out of pure ignorance chose the most suspicious and unnecessary approach. But it's not really plausible. I wish Lewis had done a little more digging.

The same wish holds for Aleynikov's claim that he only took open source code. Open source code is readily available on the Internet – that's the idea behind it. Why didn't he just plan on re-downloading the code at his new job? It's difficult to buy the idea that it would be easier for Aleynikov to transfer the files to a third-party server, later retrieve them, and then "disentangle" all the Goldman proprietary code.

---

[63] It's a little unclear where Aleynikov sent the code. Lewis first says he emailed the code to himself, then later mentions a website. Neither approach would leave a password in the bash history.

Should Aleynikov have gone to prison? It seems extremely harsh to me. But perhaps Lewis shouldn't have given him a "get out of jail free" card so easily.

CHAPTER 6:

HOW TO TAKE BILLIONS FROM WALL STREET

I like the ambiguity of Lewis' title for this chapter.

No really. Because when you read the chapter a second time, you wonder to whom he is really referring. There is a lot of hand-wringing about Ryan giving up a $910,000 annual salary (plus bonus) and Katsuyama giving up his $2 million a year job (plus bonus) to start a new exchange called IEX. Lewis tells us that it's not about the money, it's a moral crusade.

But, as Lewis admits, "if this new stock exchange flourished, its founders stood to make money – maybe a lot of money." How much? How much exactly is a stock exchange worth? The two largest exchange groups, CME Group and Intercontinental Exchange, are worth about $20 billion apiece. While IEX would likely never grow as large as these two giants, perhaps they might match a smaller exchange like BATS, valued somewhere between a half a billion and a billion dollars. One way or another, somebody may take billions from Wall Street.[64]

Of course, one could still have a crusade where one's principles happen to align with massive financial gain. This is, in fact, the story

---

[64] In Chapter 7 Lewis tells us that, before IEX even opens for business, Katsuyama rebuffs "an overture...to buy IEX for hundreds of millions of dollars." Not a bad return for a few years' work, but apparently not enough.

of the original crusades one thousand years ago. Like the original crusaders, once Katsuyama and his band launched, they were fully committed in a way they hadn't been at RBC. Their thesis of high-frequency front-running had been *part* of the story at RBC – it drove sales for Thor – but most of their day-to-day work was unrelated. If they finally got a look at the actual market data and it turned out they were wrong about high-frequency trading, they would still keep their million-dollar-a-year jobs.

But once they went all-in on IEX, there was no turning back. The whole premise of the venture was that one needed protection from high-frequency traders. You simply couldn't raise millions of dollars to build an anti-high-frequency exchange, and later admit that pretty much all high-frequency trading was O.K. Whatever the experimental data turned out to show, they were now fully committed to their conclusion. It was part of their business, and part of their story. As Lewis embeds himself in IEX's offices, one wonders to what extent the conclusion of his book was preordained by the untested beliefs of the guys he sat next to. As Lewis admits later in the book, "[Wall Street firms] are more likely than they once were to seek to shape any story told about them."

The Birth of IEX: History Repeating

At this point in the narrative, Lewis has outlined a number of problems that he sees in the market: excessive fragmentation among market centers; co-location; dark pools; order types like mid-point pegs that permit gaming in dark pools; and, of course, high-frequency traders. The solution is IEX.

IEX is a new dark pool (one of more than fifty market centers, for those keeping count) that will offer co-location (but with a delay of 0.350 milliseconds) that offers mid-point peg orders (in its dark pool), open to high-frequency traders (who apparently are no longer all bad).[65] It's not exactly revolutionary – pretty much every one of these elements exists in some shape or form on one of the other fifty places to trade – but that's not the point. The point is that it delivers confidence, and that is quite important.

At the bottom of it all, confidence is really what this policy debate is all about, since the evidence seems scant at best. Opponents of high-frequency trading love the idea of IEX because they think it kills high-frequency trading. But proponents of high-frequency trading should love it too: even if you believe it is trying to solve a problem that doesn't exist, there is real value in everyone feeling confident that the problem is solved and we can move on.

From that perspective, I hope that IEX gains traction.

Maker-Taker: Bait or Business?

"The maker-taker system of fees and kickbacks used by all of the exchanges was simply a method for paying the big Wall Street banks to screw the investors whose interests they were meant to guard. The rebates were the bait in the high-frequency traders' flash traps."

If we are to believe that the rebates are the "bait" in a "flash trap" – whatever that is – then what should we make of the exchanges that do not provide rebates to those taking liquidity?

Recall that some exchanges would pay Katsuyama to trade against their quote (i.e. a rebate for taking liquidity) and others would charge him (i.e. a fee for taking liquidity). Are the exchanges without this rebate "bait" then free of high-frequency predators? As it turns out, none of the top five exchanges rebate liquidity takers on a regular basis. Simply put, the "bait" isn't there.

---

[65] See http://www.iextrading.com. Co-location is offered via cross-connects in same data center as the BATS and Direct Edge exchanges.

It's not possible that high-frequency traders are using rebates as bait on NASDAQ, NYSE, or the other big exchanges to attract liquidity takers. It's not possible because these exchanges don't pay rebates for taking liquidity.

More broadly, it seems that Lewis is considering it nefarious for an exchange to attract business by offering a better deal to those taking liquidity – for, in his model, the only rationale for attracting liquidity takers is to lure them into a "flash trap." Suffice to say that the pricing used by IEX – $0.0009 per share for takers – is far more attractive to a taker than the pricing on any of the major exchanges. Applying Lewis' logic, this is just another kickback to the big banks (all of whom are on IEX), and IEX is one big "flash trap." If it seems logically inconsistent, that's because it is.

Realistically, different pricing models are just that: different pricing models. They are set by the exchange to attract business. To claim that high-frequency puppet-masters dictate these pricing structures to the exchanges doesn't make sense in the case of IEX, NASDAQ, NYSE, or anyone else.

Order Types That Confuse Michael Lewis

Lewis correctly notes that there is a bewildering array of order types in the markets. While each order type may be useful to someone, the overall effect is that they create a rat's nest of complexity that only gets worse over time.

Unfortunately, Lewis tries to explain the function of these order types by arguing backward from his forgone conclusion that every particular order type must be some high-frequency trader's trick. This simply isn't the way it works. Exchanges propose new order types at the request of their customers. They submit these plans to the SEC, who, after a period of public comment, either approves or rejects them. For example, the mid-point peg order type (which IEX uses) was created at the request of big bank traders like Katsuyama, not by high-frequency traders. I happen to think this order type is a very bad idea for anyone who likes certainty about price or execution, but many people love mid-point pegs. This is why the exchanges provide the choice to investors.

To whit, Katsuyama's IEX dark pool recently added another order type, the "primary peg." I suspect that this wasn't created to "hardwire into the exchange's brain the interests of high-frequency traders," but rather to respond to customer requests for another choice. Regardless, Lewis clings to this assumption that every order type must somehow channel the interests of high-frequency traders – and, predictably, he has a hard time consistently describing these interests, since he opted not to interview any high-frequency traders for his book.

For example, Lewis describes some unnamed order type for which "the purpose seemed to be to prevent a high-frequency trader from buying a small number of shares from an investor who was about to crush the market with a huge sale." This caught my eye because four chapters ago Lewis explained how he thinks high-frequency front-running works: a high-frequency trader buys a small number of shares from an investor who is placing a huge sale. In this chapter, Lewis tells us that these high-frequency traders actually want exactly the opposite. Which is it? I tend to believe that his new explanation, which contradicts his front-running scam, is the more plausible: market-makers with orders resting in the markets are easy targets, and they don't want to get crushed by a big trader like Katsuyama.

After some digging, an astute trader pointed out to me that there actually was an order type similar to what Lewis describes on one particular market, called a "PL Select" order: it would permit one's order to avoid trading with certain types and sizes of other orders at the same price. This is absurd, and it's good that Lewis shines a light on it. That's not the way markets are supposed to work. For the record, high-frequency traders feel the same way that Lewis does on this one.

Things don't get much clearer as Lewis delves into two specific named order types in detail, the Post Only order and the Hide Not Slide order.

Post Only. Lewis completely misses the purpose of the Post Only order, but he describes the order fairly accurately: "I want to buy a hundred shares of Proctor & Gamble at eighty dollars a share, but only if I am on the passive side of the trade, where I can collect a rebate from the exchange."[66] He never takes the time to ask why this might be necessary. It's a curious question, worth probing.

First, why doesn't the trader already know if he is taking or adding liquidity? Shouldn't this trader already know whether or not an order to buy P&G at $80.00 will cross an existing offer to sell P&G at $80.00? Doesn't his perfect market data tell him exactly what the current offering price is? The answer is, of course, no. High-frequency traders, just like (almost) everyone else, know that there is no perfect view of the market. Further, the market can change when their order is en route to the exchange.

A Post Only order is only useful if the trader is trying to set a *better* bid than the current best bid. For example, the trader might submit a Post Only bid to buy at $80.01, hoping to provide a new best price to the market, but unwilling to do so if he has to incur a fee for accidentally taking liquidity. This order type isn't useful or necessary if the price of the order isn't close to or better than the current best bid in the market. If the market for P&G is currently $80.00 – 80.02, there's no reason to submit a Post Only bid to buy at $79.90, since there are many bids ahead of it at better prices.

Second, why is the fee/rebate important? Market-making is an extremely low-margin business, and trading fees are the largest cost. Typically, an exchange rebates $0.002 cents for providing liquidity and charges $0.003 cents for taking liquidity. In the ideal scenario, the market-maker sets a new best bid on the market of $80.01. When

---

[66] In most variations on this order type, the exchange would immediately reject the order if it would remove/take liquidity.

someone sells shares to him at his new price, he earns a rebate of $0.002 per share. If, however, his attempt to set a new best bid at $80.01 accidentally collides with somebody trying to set a new best offer at the same price, he immediately pays $0.003 per share. His expected profits have dropped by half a penny per share.

This doesn't sound like a lot, but market-makers typically make a lot less than half a penny per share. Thus, the accidental collision turned a potential small profit into a bigger loss. It usually gets even worse. Why did his bid collide with a new lower offer? The market is now nudging downward. At best, he can sell the shares at the same price he bought them, locking in the loss caused by trading fees. It's more likely that he'll wind up selling the shares at a lower price, adding insult to injury by piling on a trading loss on top of his trading fees.

Taking a broader view, the idea of the Post Only order is to mitigate these risks. By mitigating the risks of unexpectedly paying away one's profit in fees, market-makers are incentivized to make better markets. If the Post Only order allows a market-maker to improve the price by a penny, that's one penny more in the pocket of the investor who is buying from him. Thus, the beneficiaries of this order type not only include competitive market-makers, but also folks who take liquidity, like Katsuyama.[67]

Post Only, Hide Not Slide. A "Post-Only, Hide Not Slide" order is quite similar to a "Post-Only" order, with a small twist. Lewis goes through some bewildering, somewhat nonsensical contortions to describe the order, so perhaps a more straightforward explanation will help.

---

[67] Does everybody win then? No. The loser is the market-maker who had the *previous* best bid (at $80.00 in this example). He could have made an extra penny per share from a liquidity taker's market order, but the more competitive market-maker takes this business away by accepting a lower profit margin. For those keeping score, it's approximately: old market-maker zero, new market-maker ½, investor one.

Let us assume that the market for P&G is 80.01 – 80.02. A trader places a Post-Only order to buy P&G shares at $80.02. However, it is not possible to add liquidity or "post" at $80.02 since there is an existing offer at that price. Thus, the Post-Only order is immediately rejected by the exchange. When this happens, the trader could simply re-send the order, in hopes that perhaps the offer at $80.02 has just disappeared and their bid will now be the new, best bid in the market.

However, re-sending the order to the exchange is inefficient for everyone. As an alternative, the exchange can hold on to the order until it can actually be "live." There are two ways to do so. First, the exchange can "slide" the price down to a valid live price, such as $80.01 in this case. Second, the exchange can "hide" the order until such time as it could be valid. In this case, the order would be inactive until the offer at $80.02 disappeared, making room for a new best bid at $80.02. After that time, the order would be live, just like any other order in the market, and it would provide a new best price for the market.

This order type not only reduces the number of orders sent to and from the exchange – an issue which Lewis complains about on the next page – it also helps slower market participants compete with faster participants, since there isn't a race to submit the first Post-Only order that isn't rejected. You probably noticed it already, but, just like the Post-Only order, it also creates a better price for any investor coming into the market, saving him a penny.

Lewis cooks his example slightly differently. His hypothetical trader looks at the market of 80.01 – 80.02 and decides to place an order to buy at $80.03, Post-Only Hide Not Slide. Lewis tells us that "he did this not because he wanted to buy shares" but instead he wants to "cut in line ahead of" "a real investor, channeling capital to productive enterprise." I can't really speak to how Lewis divines who the other side of the trade is, let alone that it is "a real investor, channeling capital to productive enterprise." I would also point out it's rather absurd to claim that somebody wants to buy so badly that they "cut in line," and to simultaneously claim that they don't actually want to buy.

Lewis' punch line is this: if another trader places an order to buy all the shares offered at $80.02, the first guy who bid to purchase at $80.03 will be ahead of a bid for $80.02! Amidst the shock and indignation, Lewis buries the fact that the best-priced bid *has* to be the first one in line. This is the law, but it is also common sense: would you tell the next seller that she has to accept the inferior bid price of $80.02 for her sale when there is a better price of $80.03 available?

As with most of these examples, there are other flaws. In this case, the market after the big purchase at $80.02 would likely be 80.02 – 80.03.[68] Thus, the Post-Only-Hide-Not-Slide bid for $80.03 would still be hidden, since its price would cross the offer at $80.03. So, actually, Lewis' big buyer would be first in line.

Here, though, Lewis is barreling to the punch line and the only way to (almost) get there is by making the Post-Only-Hide-Not-Slide unrealistically priced.

Summing it up, either (a) the Hide-Not-Slide becomes first in line because it's the best price in the market, or (b) the Hide-Not-Slide is not first in line. Either way, the market handles it fairly and accurately, even if the book doesn't.

Orders: What Trades Are Made Of

> *"Most of the order types were designed to not trade, or at least to discourage trading...[T]he high-frequency traders wanted to obtain information, as cheaply and risklessly as possible, about the behavior and intentions of stock market investors. That is*

---

[68] In virtually every stock there are offers to buy and sell at prices beyond the best bid and best offer, often for much greater quantities. This is called "depth" of liquidity.

why, though they made only half of all trades in the U.S. stock market, they submitted more than 99 percent of the orders: Their orders were a tool for divining information about ordinary investors."

Every order type in the markets consists of two parts: the intention to trade, and the conditions under which one will trade.[69]

Every order can result in a trade. Traders and investors use the conditions attached to a trade to manage the risk of getting something they don't want after the order leaves their control. For example, a limit order specifies the worst price at which one is willing to transact. Almost every order also has a time component, specifying whether the order must execute immediately (or be rejected), remain in the market only until canceled, or remain until the end of the day. Each of these conditions provides a tool for traders and investors to manage the risk associated with their order. Providing such tools to manage risk permits more precise pricing and a more efficient market.

For example, suppose I asked you today to predict exactly how much you will spend on gasoline for your car all next year – and I tell you that, not only can you not change your number, but I will make you pay that amount if and only if it is too high! This deal presents tremendous risk for you. Obviously, you'll pick a number so low and so far off that it is worthless. However, if we agreed that you could adjust your number under certain conditions, you might choose a slightly more realistic number. Being able to add conditions lets you manage the risk, and you can provide a better price.

What if we then agree that you can cancel our agreement at any time, and re-negotiate at another number? Suddenly, your risk is dramatically reduced. You can closely track your actual usage and update your number based on the latest information. With enough flexibility in pricing and timing, we can negotiate and strike a deal.

---

[69] Even a market order isn't without conditions – exchanges will not honor a market order if the execution price falls outside of prescribed norms.

So it goes with the markets. It's no coincidence that markets have become much more cost efficient as market-makers have been able to update their prices more rapidly. It's also no coincidence that as prices became more precise, they required more orders to manage. If all prices were rounded to the nearest dollar, they'd seldom change and new orders would be few and far between. But today stocks are priced to the penny, and this greater precision requires more frequent orders to accurately reflect the current value of the stock. It seems obvious, but one reason there were fewer orders submitted in the markets fifteen years ago is that there were few prices to choose from – everything was priced in fractions of a dollar instead of pennies.

High-frequency traders do submit a lot of orders. They do so not because they are a tool for divining information about ordinary investors.[70] They do so because their margins are so small that they must micro-manage every single price. They know that every order they submit may result in a trade, and they have to work frantically to ensure that those trades occur at the right price.

Quote stuffing. One claim frequently heard, although absent from *Flash Boys*, is that high-frequency traders submit extra orders to "stuff" or "jam" the exchanges, hoping that this will slow down the exchange just long enough to disadvantage their competitors. Curiously, this claim is most often made by technology vendors selling very fast market data processing products, and not by those competitors that are supposedly disadvantaged by it. The other supposed victims, the exchanges, don't seem that concerned either – perhaps because they have a simple remedy. For as long as I can remember, the exchanges have monitored the ratio of "orders to trades" for all participants. If any particular broker submits too

---

[70] Incidentally, most market orders from ordinary investors execute in a single trade – it's over and done with before anyone could "divine" information from it.

many orders (and it does happen), the exchange immediately detects this and warns the broker. If the broker doesn't heed the warning, they are kicked off the exchange. It almost seems too simple to be true. But that's how it works, and that's one reason why nobody makes a living "spamming" exchanges.

The other reason is that, like most of these alleged scams, it would just be bad business. Putting aside the risk of (a) getting kicked off the exchange, and (b) being fined by the SEC and barred from the industry, it just doesn't make business sense to destabilize the market upon which you are trading.

According to quote-stuffing conspiracists, the idea of such a scheme is that the destabilizer knows trouble is coming and can somehow avoid it. Technologically, this simply isn't possible. Market data contains information comingled from all market participants, and thus the destabilizer could never skip processing their "spam," because they would risk missing real activity from other participants.[71] Even if this were possible – and it's not – the destabilizer wouldn't be able to rely on using the exchange to lock in any profits because they *just destabilized the exchange*. Last, but not least, the premise in such a scenario is that the destabilizer would be the only firm with systems that are fast enough to handle the overload – which begs the question of why they wouldn't already be making their money based on that speed, instead of risking regulatory sanction.

---

[71] Specifically, I've heard speculation that someone would submit fifty orders and rapidly cancel them, and then skip processing the next fifty changes in market data (knowing them to be their own orders) to gain a slight edge in speed. It doesn't work that way. Those fifty orders still have to be processed anyway. Even if they could be skipped, one wouldn't be sure that another person's order wasn't mixed into the batch. Moreover, if you miss a single order, subsequent processing is often thrown off for the rest of the day. Overall, it's a rather brainless idea.

In sum, there's not any credible rationale for a "spamming" or "quote stuffing" conspiracy, and there is a self-correcting mechanism in the exchanges as an added protection.

An Amazingly Brief Taxonomy of Predatory Behavior

"As they worked through the order types, they created a taxonomy of predatory behavior in the stock market."

If we are to believe the narrative, the two Puzzle Masters divine the three pillars of the high-frequency trading con solely on the basis of reading order type descriptions published on the SEC website. IEX isn't operational at this point in the narrative, so there couldn't have been an opportunity to observe any high-frequency traders on their platform. There probably wasn't even any market data from other exchanges. Apparently, though, reading the order type descriptions on the web was sufficient for them to conjure up three predatory schemes:

1) Electronic front-running
2) Rebate arbitrage
3) Slow-market arbitrage

We've already debunked the front-running conspiracy in Chapter 3. Let's evaluate the other two "grotesquely unfair" activities. As a preliminary matter, note that Lewis terms both of these "arbitrage." This is a bit unusual since arbitrage is not typically considered grotesque or unfair. Arbitrage is usually defined as buying something on one market and selling it on another market for a slight profit. Economists view arbitrage as generally benign, since it keeps prices roughly equal across markets, benefiting customers of those markets. To whit, in Chapter 7, Lewis spends a paragraph praising various forms of arbitrage as "good and benign." Bearing this in mind, Lewis sets a high bar for himself to demonstrate that these particular forms of arbitrage are not good and benign, but are instead grotesquely unfair and predatory.

Rebate arbitrage. Lewis defines this as "using the new complexity to game the seizing of whatever kickbacks the exchange offered without actually providing the liquidity that the kickback was presumably meant to entice." One can either view this definition as circular or self-contradictory. Either way, it's meaningless. Lewis declines to provide an example, or even another sentence about it.

Briefly, though, it bears repeating that any rebates paid for adding liquidity are only paid when a trade occurs. Thus, it's hard to see any valid argument that the rebate was paid (or "seized") without providing liquidity.

Slow-market arbitrage. Lewis illustrates thusly: "Say, for instance, the market for P&G shares is 80-80.01, and buyers and sellers sit on both sides on all of the exchanges. A big seller comes in on the NYSE and knocks the price down to 79.98-79.99. High-frequency traders buy on NYSE at $79.99 and sell on all the other exchanges at $80, before the market officially changes. This happened all day, every day, and generated more billions of dollars a year than the other strategies combined."

Actually, this can't happen all day, or on any day. Yet again, this is impossible – by design.

Recall that Regulation NMS contains a rule called "trade-through protection." Trade-through prevents a big seller on one exchange from "trading-through" better bids on other exchanges. In this case, the big seller on the NYSE is prohibited from selling his shares at $79.99, which would be a lower price than the bids on all of the other exchanges. Better still, this rule is always enforced before the trade occurs – no after-the-fact investigations required – as the NYSE has programmed its software to automatically reject the illegal portion of his order.

The main rationale behind this rule is to protect everyone on the other exchanges that is willing to buy at a better price. They are advertising the best price in the markets, and our markets are prioritized by price.[72] To a certain extent, this also protects the big seller from making a stupid mistake and selling for less than he needs to. Broadly, if someone could ignore the best prices on other exchanges, there wouldn't really be a national market system at all.

The upshot is that the example Lewis provides is impossible. The trade-through rule prevents exactly what Lewis describes. It is built into the programming of the exchanges and enforced automatically. Looking back, Lewis mocked the Post-Only and Hide-Not-Slide orders because he found them impossible to understand. In light of the trade-through rule, they make perfect sense. Sometimes traders are willing to trade-through the best bid or offer, but they are prohibited from doing so. These order types are requests to the exchange to let them trade at those prices as soon as it is legal to do so. Had Lewis understood trade-through rules and these order types (or spoken to a trader, or a compliance officer, or a regulator), this would have been crystal clear.

Given the impossibility of this scheme, the only question remaining about "slow-market arbitrage," then, is how the Puzzle Masters determined that "[t]his happened all day, every day, and generated more billions of dollars a year than the other strategies combined." The idea that the Puzzle Masters computed any credible estimate of the profits of this impossible strategy based on order type descriptions is, well, even more incredible than the original idea that they divined top-secret trading strategies based on the same information. One could speculate how Lewis arrived at this number, but since he doesn't seem to care enough to provide any details, and

---

[72] For practical reasons, only the best bid and best offer are protected.

since the premise upon which it rests is impossible, it's not worth pursuing.

One would expect the taxonomy of predatory behavior to be the rhetorical climax of this would-be exposé, but the one paragraph dedicated to it lacks a single compelling argument. It seems like Lewis just gave up. Indeed, in the next paragraph, he even trades in his crumbling "high-frequency trading is bad" mantra for the uncontroversial argument that predatory behavior is bad: "anyway, it wasn't high-frequency trading in itself that was pernicious; it was its predations."

Confidence From a Solution that Doesn't Solve a Problem That Doesn't Exist

The challenge, as Lewis sees it, is for IEX to make sure that "honest investors with a lot of stock to sell might collide with honest investors who had a lot of stock to buy." In case you mistakenly thought that you were the "honest investor" he had in mind, you're not. This crusade is about making sure that someone buying "a million shares of P&G" – that's $80 million worth of stock – can do so comfortably. You're not the honest investor Lewis has in mind, the hedge funds presidents are.

I apologize in advance for this spoiler: from what we've heard since IEX's launch, and since the publication of the book, IEX appears to be free of high-frequency trading predation.[73]

It's reasonable to assume, then, that either (a) their solution makes these alleged high-frequency predations impossible, or (b) their solution doesn't make these alleged high-frequency predations impossible, but they are so rare or otherwise implausible that they

---

[73] As of this date, I have not seen Katsuyama discuss any such high-frequency predation on IEX in any of his numerous appearances in the press. Admittedly, it is possible that this is occurring and IEX is keeping quiet, but I find it highly unlikely.

wouldn't occur anyway. Perhaps examining the IEX solution will indicate which explanation is more likely.

Randomized Delay. Their approach to "solving" the problem reveals much about what IEX still doesn't know about how markets function. For example, the idea of a randomized delay in matching trade is discarded because "[t]he Puzzle Masters instantly spotted the problem: Any decent HFT firm would simply buy huge numbers of lottery tickets – to increase its chances of being the 100-share sell order that collided with the massive buy order." This is the sort of strategy that can only be imagined by somebody who has never traded. In Chapter 3 we examined how "pinging" was a guaranteed way to lose money, fast: executing a single 100 share trade doesn't reveal anything about how large an order, if any, your counterparty may still have, and guessing is very expensive. This "lottery ticket" strategy is a way to make a bad strategy even worse.

For one, the would-be predator is likely to collide completely with the entire massive buy order, when supposedly all he wanted to do was trade once to divine a nugget of information that would somehow be used to front-run. If he submits 100 "lottery ticket" orders to sell 100 shares each, that totals 10,000 shares. His purchases of lottery tickets would completely wipe out a buy order for 10,000 shares. In the end, he would have sold 10,000 shares, not 100 shares, and he still wouldn't know the size of the other order! Worse still, the randomized delay means that he doesn't even know how much market risk he has taken on until the last order comes back. If this is a lottery, every ticket is a losing one.

In fact, the only winner in the lottery would be the big buyer, who completely filled his order to buy *at the price he wanted.* That is, ostensibly, the goal. So why not do it? If the front-running theory is bogus (as I have argued), there is no race for a lottery ticket. If it is valid, the lottery ticket race creates the desired goal anyway. So why not?

Puzzle Master Francis ultimately decides that it's a bad idea that would be "massively increasing quote traffic for every move." Is this really why they discarded the idea? As mentioned previously, exchanges are free to set policies on order submission. If a market participant violates those policies, they can be removed from the market. So this explanation doesn't hold water either.

In the end, the problem with random delays is a business one: it makes the market far riskier for *everyone* to trade upon. Unnecessary delays are bad enough, but the added risk can be managed if one accepts lessened efficiency (i.e. worse prices). Introducing a random element makes risk management far more difficult since one cannot predict whether or not a trade has actually occurred within a given time span. That's a hard sell for your customers. Perhaps this is the real reason that IEX didn't opt for a randomized delay. On the other hand, it sounds much more clever to construct an (implausible) high-frequency straw man and blame that instead.

Fixed Delay. The solution ultimately chosen by IEX is to add a delay of 350 microseconds to every order. While this would be trivial to implement in software, they opt to coil thirty-eight miles of fiber-optic cable for each participant instead. It's not necessary, but it's brilliant marketing.

Lewis tells us that this delay must be (1) long enough to "beat HFT in a race to any other shares available in the marketplace at the same price," and (2) "long enough, also, for IEX, each time a share price moved on any exchange, to process the change, and to move the prices of any orders resting on it, so that they didn't get picked off." Apparently the magic number is a mere 320 microseconds – "the time it took them, in the worst case, to send a signal to the exchange farthest from them, the NYSE in Mahwah. Just to be sure, they rounded it up to 350 microseconds."

Remember the discussion in Chapter 3 about the surprising uptick in trading volume for shares of Sirius radio? Trading volume on the CBSX? Located in Chicago? That exchange is actually the exchange farthest from IEX – more than twenty times farther than the NYSE. Why, then, isn't the delay 15,000 microseconds, the time it would take to send a signal to the CBSX? Wouldn't this be doubly important, given Katsuyama and Ryan's fervent belief that high-frequency traders were using the Spread Networks fiber-optic line to front-run everyone else on the CBSX? So, why not a 15,000 microsecond delay?

The answer, again, is probably business concerns. The slowest exchanges took two or three milliseconds to process orders, and saw very little trading volume as a result. Few customers wanted to sit and watch the markets pass them by as they waited to know whether or not they had traded. And no customer would tolerate trading on a market that was ten to twenty times slower than any other market. So there had to be a balance between the marketing pitch – a delay big enough that nobody can outrun the IEX – and the legitimate business concern of actually having customers. In the end, the "solution" isn't really a solution. Despite this, it seems that no front-running is occurring through IEX.

With regards to the second goal of the delay, there is yet another problem. If they really want to be able to react more quickly than anyone else when a price changes on another exchange, they need to measure not just the network time, but *also the time of each exchange to process a new order*. The reason is this: if an evil predator causes the price to move on another exchange, he can start to race to IEX as soon as his price-changing order is submitted to the other exchange. He knows that the market data will change as a result of his order, and he doesn't need to wait for the exchange to broadcast the update, a delay that could be hundreds of microseconds or more. IEX has to wait until the other exchange broadcasts the update, by which time the evil predator would already have completed whatever dirty tricks they are afraid of on IEX. Again, the "solution" of IEX isn't really a solution.[74]

In the end it seems that (1) the tweaks implemented by IEX would not actually prevent the predatory trading that Lewis hypothesizes, but (2) there doesn't appear to be any predatory trading on IEX. This paradox could be explained two ways. Perhaps the predators are simply scared to show their stripes on IEX. Or perhaps the feared predatory trading is rare to non-existent, and it doesn't matter that IEX's defenses are illusory.

Order Types. IEX also chose to dramatically simplify the types of orders available: market, limit, and mid-point peg. This is commendable. Most importantly, it keeps their computer system relatively clean and thus reduces the chances of bugs in their matching logic. Such bugs are especially hard to detect in a dark pool where the users have no way of knowing if they were correctly matched or not. It also reduces the chances that one of their customers will shoot themselves in the foot by selecting the wrong order type.

On the other hand, permitting the mid-point peg order opens the door to the only actual problems we've seen so far: the dark pool arbitrage that Rich Gates apparently experienced on Goldman's platform. I understand that customers like the idea of this order – "It's kind of like the fair price," opines Katsuyama – but in practice they may not get the prices they expect. Caveat emptor.

---

[74] After operating throughout the period chronicled in *Flash Boys*, the CBSX closed for trading on April 30, 2014. This now solves the first problem outlined above for IEX, but the second problem remains.

Throwing Down the Gauntlet: Can HFT exist without speed and complexity?

"[IEX] did not ban but welcomed high-frequency traders who wished to trade on it. If high-frequency traders performed a valuable service in the financial markets, they should still do so, after their unfair advantages had been eliminated. Once the new stock exchange opened for business, IEX would be able to see how much of what HFT did was useful simply by watching what, if anything, high-frequency traders did on the new exchange, where predation was not possible."

There you have it: Lewis has distilled IEX into one giant experiment that will test his hypothesis. If high-frequency trading is purely a parasitic predation on the markets, IEX will see no high-frequency traders active on their platform. On the other hand, if high-frequency trading actually does perform a "valuable service," IEX will see them trading actively on the platform.

Thus, we now have an experiment to test the Lewis hypothesis. When IEX officially launches later in the book, we will see the first data and, if we are lucky, have a chance to test his hypothesis.

Shining a Light on Payment for Order Flow

I'm not a big fan of "payment for order flow." This is the term used in the industry for a business arrangement where broker A pays retail broker B to send broker B's customer orders to broker A, instead of to the public markets. I understand the arguments in favor of the practice – that customers sometimes get better prices than they would obtain in the public markets, and that it reduces costs for the customers' brokers and this is theoretically passed through to customers – but I still find it troubling. For one, I have a business relationship with my broker and I expect that broker to be responsible for executing my trades, not somebody else. I do not expect my broker to sell my order to some company that I don't know, to be executed in some dark back alley of Wall Street.

Lewis describes the situation more or less correctly.[75] If he doesn't make it clear enough how an order goes from conception to trade, hopefully this should help:

1) The broker receiving the order may try to trade against it. For your retail orders, this is rare. Either the retail broker lacks the capacity to trade against the order, or has sold this right to another broker downstream. For institutional orders, such as hedge funds or other money managers, this is much more common: brokers like Goldman, Morgan Stanley, or RBC may take the other side of the trade, if it looks profitable to them. If not, they will pass it down the chain.

2) A broker paying for the orders may try to "internalize" the order, or trade against it. Some portion of the orders originating at the receiving broker may be sold to another broker. That broker sometimes has the obligation to make sure the order is filled (either by him, or by passing it along to another market), and sometimes just has the option to fill it or not. If the order isn't filled at this time, it is passed down the chain.

3) A dark pool may execute the order. Orders not filled by the receiving broker or any broker to whom they were sold are often passed to a private dark pool where multiple brokers compete to fill the order. If there are no resting bids or offers that would fill the order when it arrives, it is sometimes passed to another dark pool (and this step is repeated). If it is not passed to another dark pool, it is passed to the public exchanges.

---

[75] The one exception is Lewis' bizarre quote of lobbyist Chris Nagy: "I've tried over the years [to find out how much money was being made by high-frequency trading.]" It's almost total paraphrase, leaving the reader to wonder what the real conversation was about, versus what Lewis wanted it to be about.

4) The public exchanges will execute anything remaining. As the public markets always have liquidity available, they are a reliable last resort. The order is virtually guaranteed to be filled on one of the exchanges.

It's important to note that at each point in this cascade, whoever fills the order is required by law to provide the customer with a price that matches or improves the best displayed price in the public markets. Theoretically, then, even though few retail orders ever hit the public exchanges, the customer doesn't appear to suffer. In practice, however, there is little oversight that these "off-exchange" activities fully adhere to the law.

More troubling still is the fact that even if everyone involved plays by the rules, there is great potential for deterioration of the public markets. If no orders from the general public ever make it to the "public markets," how public can they be? The public markets today are becoming more and more exclusively the domain of professional traders, and professional traders alone. More than a third of all shares traded never touch the public markets.[76] Ironically, the public's retail orders shunted to dark pools depend almost exclusively on the stock exchanges of which they are no longer a part.

Both an institutional mid-point peg order and a retail market order filled in a dark pool are priced based on a synthetic calculation of how that particular dark pool sees data in the public markets. Yet neither order ever participates in the public markets. The price and quantity are never displayed publicly (it's a dark pool, remember?), and when the order executes it doesn't subtract from the supply in the public markets. In short, your retail order plays no role in "price discovery," or in determining the price of the stock. Even after the fact, your order has minimal impact on future price – any trade that occurs in a dark pool needn't be reported to the public in realtime.

---

[76] For example, see "Dark Pools Take Larger Share of Trades Amid SEC Scrutiny," Sam Mamudi, Bloomberg, June 13, 2014.

It's as if you're invited to an auction where you can buy, but you can't participate in bidding for the price – only a select group of "professionals" on the other side of the room can. Whatever you say about the price is irrelevant. Remarkably, the price you receive won't even be the price at which the professionals actually bought or sold, it will merely be the synthetic composite of what the professionals *said* they might pay.

This is the danger of the current system: you get the price set by Wall Street negotiating with Wall Street, and you, and the rest of the general public, have little to no role influencing that process of price discovery.

This is extremely troubling. It's a concern shared by many in the markets, as well as regulators. The problem is that nobody knows where the "tipping point" is – the point at which so much trading takes place in dark pools, based on this synthetic price, that the real price in the public markets becomes worthless. The only point of agreement is that everyone hopes the tipping point is still far away.

Why do brokers now pay to process customer orders? It seems rather counterintuitive. Ten years ago, a retail broker had to pay to send their customer orders to a stock market. But today, that retail broker can be paid for sending their customer orders to another broker? What makes the opportunity to process a retail customer's order valuable?

Lewis proffers his theory that the value of retail stock orders is that they are slow: "High-frequency traders sought to trade as often as possible with ordinary investors, who had slower connections." He tells us that their orders are late to the market, a full second behind. Oddly, he simply leaves this explanation hanging there. He never completes the thought, perhaps because he can't.

If a retail customer sends a market order – to purchase at the current market price – it doesn't matter if it is fast, or slow. The order is given the current market price, right now at this instant. If you sent a market order at 10am and it wasn't received until 11am, it is executed at the current price in the 11am market. It doesn't matter that it took an hour to make it to the market. Market orders receive the current market price, no matter what. If a retail customer sends a limit order – to purchase at a specific price – then they are guaranteed to receive that price. Neither case hinges upon milliseconds, or even seconds for that matter.

Consider another perspective on the Lewis hypothesis: for much of the day, the market is actually quite boring. The best bid and best offer – the prices at which any market order would execute – don't change much at all. What advantage is to be had by interacting with a "slow" order that was sent a whole second ago, when the market hasn't moved in the past minute? None. The value of these orders is simply not related to speed, or lack thereof. As Katsuyama himself says in the next chapter, "I knew it was bullshit to worry about milliseconds."[77]

There is another explanation for the value of retail orders, and it's not a secret by any stretch – it's the well-known industry concept of "directional" and "non-directional" order flow. The gist is that professional traders, like hedge funds, sell when the market is dropping (or about to drop), and they buy when the market is climbing (or about to climb). This is, of course, the reason these people exist. They make money by betting that other people are wrong. In practice, this means that if you are on the other end of the trade with them – for example, you are a market-maker who has stuck his neck out with an order resting in the market – you are likely to be stuck with a losing position, just as the market starts to move. It goes without saying that this isn't a desirable business.

---

[77] To be fair, this quote comes in the context of Katsuyama defending his market's delayed executions to potential customers – it's possible that he might adopt the opposite position in other circumstances.

On the other hand, retail investors tend to place orders based on their personal desires, not based on the second-to-second movements of the market. It may be selling some shares to pay the tax bill, buying some shares for your children's college fund, or any other common financial need, but, whatever it is, you probably aren't buying shares based upon the just-released revision to the prior quarter's PPI. When you execute your trade, it's not because you think the market is about to make a dramatic move, it's simply because you want to execute a trade and get it done. Accordingly, whoever is on the other side of the trade isn't automatically stuck with a losing position. The market may go up, go down, or stay put. The trade is not necessarily a winner, but it's not necessarily a loser, either.

How then is a retail order "valuable"? It's not. It's only valuable in that a professional order is "toxic" – that's actually the industry term for directional orders — and a retail order is not. A market-maker is likely to lose money when a professional takes their liquidity. A market-maker has at least a fifty-fifty chance if a retail order takes their liquidity. The value of a retail stock order to a market-maker is simply that he's not guaranteed to lose money.

Regardless, Lewis clings to his theory that retail orders are valuable because they are (somehow) slow. In the end, he poses another quantitative "experiment" to test his hypothesis: "If the Puzzle Masters were right, and the design of IEX eliminated the advantage of speed, IEX would reduce the value of investors' stock market orders to zero. If the orders couldn't be exploited on this new exchange – if the information they contained was worthless – who would pay for the right to execute them?" Who indeed? Lewis is now doubling-down on his bet on IEX and high-frequency traders.

If he is correct and the only reason that high-frequency traders trade with retail investors is a difference in speed, then no high-frequency traders will pay IEX to trade on their market. If, however, Lewis is incorrect, and the value is not based on a difference in speed, but rather the value of non-directional orders (i.e. not getting taken for a ride on every order), then high-frequency traders may actually pay to trade on IEX. We'll soon see what happens with the IEX launch.

So, am I getting ripped off or not? A retail order handled in a dark pool is protected in almost all circumstances, provided that the dark pool obeys the law, specifically regarding trade-through rules (requiring that the customer receives as good a price or better on the dark pool as she would on the public markets) and immediacy (new orders either instantly execute against pre-existing orders, or do not).

However, these protections against manipulation are predicated on the assumption that the dark pool in question, or a broker's internalization facility as the case may be, properly handles market orders without allowing them to "rest" in their private market for even a microsecond. These protections also assume that the dark pool enforces the "best execution" requirement properly, with up-to-date and accurate information about current prices in the national markets that constrain the price that a customer market order may receive in the dark pool. With neither public disclosure of each dark pool's rules, nor adequate transparency around the executions themselves, these assumptions must be taken purely on faith. So the question becomes: do you trust Wall Street to behave when nobody is watching?

For institutional and professional traders using a mid-point peg order, the situation becomes even murkier. As described previously, this order combines the worst of market and limit orders – one loses control over the price like a market order, and one loses control over the timing like a limit order. And, as described in Chapter 4, this can lead to a scenario where said professional trader gets what he asks for, but not necessarily what he wants.

Overall, dark pools and broker internalization facilities aren't unquestionably bad, but it's hard to make a compelling case for any significant benefit. For professionals in particular, they make it easier to shoot oneself in the foot. For the public, the lack of transparency doesn't inspire confidence. And for the markets themselves, there is a legitimate question about whether or not they detract from the price discovery process.

For these reasons, I believe that the default destination for retail customer orders should always be the public markets. If customers want to "opt in" and select a dark pool or internalizer for their orders, that's fine, but it should be a choice the customer makes – not a choice that the broker makes for them.

The Impossibility of Getting Full and Precise Information

Lewis, now embedded in the offices of IEX, walks us through a discussion of how IEX might provide information to the customers of the banks about how the banks and IEX handle their orders. Providing this information is a real problem in the industry.

You can see it for yourself when you execute a trade through your retail broker. The information you get is adequate, but couldn't be called complete. It certainly can't be called precise, as you're lucky if you are provided the second at which your order was executed.

Interestingly, the problem Katsuyama is trying to solve is one that is a product of his vocation: big bank equity desks didn't provide their customers with adequate information about how their trades were handled. While Lewis implies that this obscurity is designed to mask the vast conspiracy of high-frequency trading, this problem predates Regulation NMS, high-frequency trading, and pretty much everything else in the modern markets.

One can't say for sure why equity desks at banks haven't provided more information to their customers about executions, but one possibility is that it's simply not in their interests to do so. Such information would invite the customers to comparison shop. Recall that in Chapter 2, Katsuyama charges his client a price that is five cents worse than the market in Solectron, even though he apparently expects to trade the whole block at the current market price. The client believed he was paying a quarter of a million dollars for Katsuyama's unique skill in making the trade, but if it looked like anyone could do the same – or, easier still, some computer algorithm could do it automatically – that client might be much less willing to pay hundreds of thousands to RBC. Thus, brokers have historically been rather reluctant to share the details of their trades with customers.

IEX is now fighting this unfortunate tradition, and that's a very good thing – even more so for a dark pool like IEX, who is leading by example. If transactions are going to be consummated away from the public eye, customers have a right to know exactly what happened.

Lastly, on the topic of how difficult it is to get full and precise information, it's worth touching upon Lewis' reference to Joe Saluzzi's blog post about "private trade information" being "actively broadcast" to high-frequency traders. In 2010, Saluzzi correctly pointed out that, using the market data protocols accessible to anyone (not just high-frequency traders, but brokers like himself), one could theoretically determine that two completed trades were linked to the same underlying order, provided that these orders were of a particular uncommon order type. The exchanges promptly revised their protocols and fixed the issue. Far from being "credible evidence of Big Foot," the obscurity of this issue illustrates just how far one has to stretch to allege the Big Foot conspiracy: there was no claim that the order quantity is revealed, nor the identity of the person submitting the order. Instead, the allegation was simply that the market data provided a way to link two trades that had already executed.

The reason you never heard of this is that it simply wasn't significant. Trade information is already public, and linking two trades that already occurred is neither hugely insightful, nor a breach of secrecy. Such information can, in fact, be inferred by anyone who knows that all orders must be executed based on the price and order in which they are received. Regardless, this particular bug was quickly fixed four years ago by the affected exchanges, and (almost) everybody moved on.

CHAPTER 7:

IEX LAUNCHES

Investor Confidence: Inconsistent Irrelevance

The Post-Only order type resurfaces early in this chapter, with Lewis drawing a bizarre analogy to its implementation causing the death of a race-car driver. Really.

The reader is then led to infer that either the fear of Post-Only orders, or a fiery car crash due to the use of Post-Only orders, has scared everyone away from the stock market:

> "[T]he investing public had lost faith in the U.S. stock market. Since the flash crash back in May 2010, the S&P index had risen 65 percent, and yet trading volume was down 50 percent: For the first time in history, investors' desire to trade had not risen with market prices. Before the flash crash, 67 percent of U.S. households owned stocks; by the end of 2013, only 52 percent did: the fantastic post-crisis bull market was noteworthy for how many Americans elected not to participate in it."

This is surprising for a number of reasons. Putting aside the numbers – which are actually wrong – the real surprise is why Lewis thinks people are wary of investing in the stock market today. It apparently is due to the twenty minutes of trading in 2010 known as the flash crash, and has nothing to do with losing $19.2 trillion dollars in the Financial Crisis.[78] Really? If you are one of the 99.9% of the U.S. population who doesn't watch CNBC, chances are you've barely heard of the flash crash, if at all. On the other hand, 99.9% of the population saw homes foreclosed, jobs lost, and investment accounts decimated in the Financial Crisis. Which do you think affected investor confidence more strongly?

Using the Gallup data that Lewis incorrectly employed, Reuters journalist Ben Walsh observes that stock ownership has declined *every year* since 2007.[79] The largest two drops come in the years of the Financial Crisis: from 2008 to 2009, and from 2007 to 2008.

Lewis continues with another inconsistent non sequitur, arguing that a decline in market volume indicates a decline in public confidence in the stock market. One hundred pages prior, he had first argued the opposite: one couldn't say that the increase in trading volume from 2006 to 2009 was relevant, because increases in trading volume had little relation to the actual quality of the markets. I agree with the first Michael Lewis – changes in volume don't imply changes in the quality of markets.

There's also a rather reasonable observation that if an item costs a lot more than it used to, you can't buy as many of them as you used to. To be precise, if the price of stocks increased by 65% (as Lewis tells us), and you had the same amount of dollars available, your money buys 39% fewer shares. Coincidentally, average daily trading volume in 2013 was 37% lower than in 2009.[80] In other words, people are still putting the same amount of dollars out there,

---

[78] See "The Financial Crisis Response In Charts," U.S. Treasury Department, April 2012.

[79] See "US stock ownership: Fact-checking Michael Lewis," Ben Walsh, Reuters, April 1, 2014. Walsh points out a number of errors in Lewis' statement, not the least of which is that the "67%" number is actually 56%.

[80] Average daily volume in 2009 was 9.8 billion shares; it was 6.2 billion shares in 2013. See "Volume is finally back in the stock market," Bloomberg News, February 14, 2014.

it's just that stocks have increased in value.[81] Even when Lewis tries to argue both sides of the volume argument, he's wrong.

In sum, there is no new crisis of confidence in the stock markets. If there were, it would not be due to high-frequency trading or the flash crash – relatively unknown to the general public until this book. It would be due to Michael Lewis proclaiming that the stock market is rigged on "60 Minutes."

Complexity and Instability – A Never-ending Battle

Lewis correctly points out that there have been numerous "technical errors" in the markets in the past few years. On the other hand, his claim that there have been as many errors in 2011 and 2012 as in the prior ten years is, like almost all of his claims, unsubstantiated. It also doesn't match my experience. Ten years ago there were problems too. And ten years before that. More so when only humans were involved. In fact, problems were so common that exchanges had elaborate procedures at the end of each day where trading clerks frantically tried to match "tickets" (i.e. little scraps of paper) to make sure each side of each trade was in agreement. A day with zero mistakes was a rarity.

The difference today is that (a) everyone expects 100.00% accuracy, and (b) critics of the system are quick to jump on any problem, no matter what the size. Every system, no matter how well designed, will have some technical problem. Complicated systems are more likely to have problems, but even a "simple" stock market will face its share of problems at some point (and this includes IEX). Even if your systems are perfect, you have to depend on the outside world at some point, and there's the guy with a backhoe who digs up

---

[81] Retail investors made more trades in April 2014 than any other month on record. See "Small Investors Show No Fear," Businessweek, June 2, 2014.

your network line, a power grid failure, or somebody at your data center accidentally pulling out the wrong cable.[82]

Interestingly, the diversity of the modern markets contributes both to the perception of frequent problems and to the actual insignificance of those problems. Twenty-five years ago, virtually all trading in IBM occurred on one single exchange, orchestrated by a single "specialist" on the floor. Having a single point-of-failure wasn't exactly a model of redundancy, but in the era predating the ubiquity of CNBC and the existence of Twitter, it wasn't news if there was a problem trading IBM for a few hours.

Today there are eleven exchanges and a multitude of market-makers. Far from a single point-of-failure, there are numerous alternatives in almost any given disaster scenario. What Lewis doesn't tell the reader is that when one exchange has a problem, the market simply relies on the other ten.

This was, in fact, part of the design of Regulation NMS. It's a brilliant realization that one can never prevent every type of failure, but perhaps one can create a system that is robust enough to continue to function properly when one or more single parts fail. If this sounds familiar, it's the same principle on which the Internet was designed.

This design is not the only way in which the SEC has tried to address complexity and technological risk in the markets. Since the flash crash, the SEC has implemented circuit breakers in individual stocks to prevent sudden price swings. It has created unified market-wide circuit breakers to pause trading if the broader markets again drop unexpectedly. It has required all broker-dealers to implement a suite of risk controls that assess and approve every single order before it is sent in the markets. It has worked with the exchanges and the SIP consortium to improve the reliability and performance of their technology. Not content with that, it has proposed to codify

---

[82] These are just a handful of actual problems that I've encountered that were completely outside of our control.

requirements on capacity planning, stress testing, disaster recovery, and regular systems testing through Regulation SCI. It's not perfect, but it's progress.

Interestingly, these initiatives are not targeted at particular business models, but rather the processes and technologies that have caused or might cause actual problems. When critics say that high-frequency trading must be curbed because they fear the risk of a trading algorithm run amok, one wonders if they are really concerned about trading algorithms – which are used by every professional on Wall Street – or about competitive business models.[83]

So has the demon of complexity been slain? The many changes of the past four years would probably prevent another flash crash like that of May 2010. The problems underlying that event have been addressed through multiple solutions. But one can never eliminate every risk. If you listen carefully, those who decry the stability of today's markets aren't even attempting to offer a solution. They recognize that there is no perfect solution to be offered. Sometimes, they even grudgingly admit that the system they are criticizing is still better than anything in the past.

Lewis won't allow himself such an admission, but he does have to admit that his designated expert on instability, Zoran Perkov, "liked to argue that there were actually fewer, not more, 'technical glitches' in 2012 than there had been in 2006."

---

[83] It bears repeating that the SEC and CFTC cited an ineptly executed trading algorithm as the triggering event of the flash crash of May 2010. The trading algorithm was operated by a trader at a mutual fund company. Reasonably, neither regulator proposed curbing mutual funds; instead they focused on better risk controls governing the use of such algorithms.

Quoting Academic Research that Disproves Front-Running

In a footnote Lewis cites academic research by Adam Clark-Joseph that he says shows how high-frequency traders might lose money on stock market orders in order to make more money elsewhere. He obviously didn't read the paper for two reasons. The first reason is that it refers to the futures markets, not the stock market.

The second reason is that, as I mentioned in the preface, this paper dismisses Lewis' entire front-running hypothesis out of hand:

> "One possibility is that HFTs merely react to public information faster than everyone else...a second possibility is that the HFTs simply front-run coming demand when they can predict future orders. However, I find neither of these hypotheses to be consistent with the data."[84]

In other words, this research, cited by Lewis at the conclusion of his book, contradicts everything he has said on the prior 200 pages. The researcher tested the data to see if the trades matched a front-running model. His conclusion was quite clear.

Hedge Funds: Keeping Your Best Interests At Heart

> *"The sixteen investors [in IEX] controlled roughly $2.6 trillion in stock market investments among them, or roughly 20 percent of the entire U.S. market."*

As many reviewers have pointed out, one of the more surprising elements of *Flash Boys* is the literary gymnastics required to convince the reader that the complaints of big bank equities traders and hedge fund managers are, in fact, our complaints. Even though your individual stock orders aren't impacted by high-frequency

---

[84] See "Exploratory Trading," Adam Clark-Joseph, Job Market Paper. January 13, 2013.

trading, Lewis argues, if your hedge fund thinks it has a problem, then you (and the American public) have a problem too.

This may be somewhat true for the 1% – only if you happen to have a minimum net worth of $1 million (not including the value of your house) are you allowed to invest in a hedge fund. Trying to make hedge funds relevant to the 99%, Lewis explains that your pension fund just might have a fraction of its portfolio invested in a hedge fund – so if you work for the government, or are one of the 18% of employees in private industry that have a pension plan, he thinks you should be rooting for the hedge funds.[85]

Of course, the absurdity of this argument cuts both ways. Yes, some pensions have likely invested in the hedge funds that are complaining about high-frequency trading firms, but many of those same pensions are also invested in high-frequency trading firms. For example, more than a third of high-frequency trading behemoth KCG / Getco is owned by institutions and mutual funds.[86] CalPERS and CalSTRS, two of the largest pension funds in the country, own stakes in privately held high-frequency firms as part of their private equity portfolio.[87] If an investment by a mutual fund or pension fund automatically makes our interests the same as those who the fund has invested in, we are then aligned as much with the high-frequency trading firms as we are with the hedge funds.

What are those interests anyway? Why do some hedge funds have a problem with high-frequency trading when the Vanguards of the world do not? The answer is that Vanguard doesn't day-trade, and those hedge funds do. Companies like Vanguard invest for the long-term and prize efficient markets, which improve the performance of their long-term investments. Most hedge funds, on

[85] See "The Last Private Industry Pension Plans," Bureau of Labor Statistics, Department of Labor, January 3, 2013.

[86] See Yahoo Finance, KCG Major Holders as/of March 31, 2014.

[87] See CalPERS PE Program Fund Performance Review as/of December 31, 2013. Also see CalSTRS PE Program Fund Performance Review as/of September 30, 2013.

the other hand, make their money by trying to trade small, fleeting opportunities in the markets. If this sounds similar to what high-frequency trading firms do, that's not a coincidence.

Hedge-funds, using computer algorithms to trade stocks frequently, were the original high-frequency traders, and some of them don't like the new competition. Hedge fund performance has declined in the past decade, in a mirror image of high-frequency trading's growth.[88] Of course, some hedge funds continue to perform well, and, coincidentally, don't seem to mind high-frequency trading. Greenlight Capital, one of the hedge funds lionized in Lewis' book *The Big Short* and one of the investors in IEX, recently wrote to its customers that the schemes alleged in *Flash Boys* "don't significantly impact us."[89]

In the end, then, let's not pretend that just because some hedge fund managers claim to believe something, the rest of us must believe it. As you'd expect, they are looking out for their own interests, not ours.

Conspiracy of Press Releases

"The game is now clear to me," Brad said. "There's not a press release I don't understand."

Lewis presents us with a curious standard: if one can understand press releases, it qualifies one as an expert in capital market microstructure. More curious still is the understanding of press releases that is required.

Apparently, every press release is a coded message from the high-frequency conspiracy. According to Lewis, NASDAQ's missive

---

[88] See "High-frequency trading hurts hedge funds – not you," Chuck Jaffe, MarketWatch, May 5, 2014.

[89] See Greenlight Capital letter to investors, dated April 22, 2014.

on their August 22, 2013, outage – "what they said was a technical glitch in the SIP" – wasn't really about a technical glitch in the SIP. Lewis tells us that the outage was really caused by high-frequency traders because NASDAQ spent money on co-location facilities. Specifically, NASDAQ spent money on power supplies and cooling systems – both necessary to make sure one's computers don't blow up or melt down, causing system outages – and "cross-connects," which is a term of art that simply means "network cables."[90] Although Lewis previously implied that co-location is a huge profit center for NASDAQ, here he implies the exact opposite: co-location somehow siphoned off revenue needed to pay for SIP development, resulting in this particular outage.

As I mentioned earlier, the SIP is sadly undermanned. This isn't because NASDAQ has failed to allocate any profits from co-location to maintaining the SIP. It's because the SIP was basically structured as a consortium funded by all the exchanges, none of which have an incentive to pay an additional penny to maintain it. So nobody does.

It's remarkable the number of contortions necessary to morph every press release into an indictment of high-frequency trading. The next example is no different. A press release announces that after the merger of BATS and Direct Edge, both exchanges will remain open. Lewis explains that, "To Brad the reason was obvious: The exchanges were both at least partially owned by high-frequency trading firms, and, from the HFT point of view, the more exchanges the better." Perhaps he should have read a few other press releases first.

In 2006, the NYSE acquired the Archipelago Exchange. In 2007 NASDAQ purchased the Boston Stock Exchange. Later that year, NASDAQ purchased the Philadelphia Stock Exchange. In 2008, the NYSE acquired the American Stock Exchange. In each acquisition, the acquired exchange remained open. Was this because the NYSE and

---

[90] IEX, and pretty much every other market center, provide these features to customers, as does any data center hosting non-financial companies.

NASDAQ were owned by high-frequency traders? No. They are public companies – it says so at the bottom of their press releases.

When exchanges merge, they usually consolidate sales and "back-office" functions, and sometimes even trading platforms. However, they continue to operate separate markets because this permits them to capture different market segments through different pricing models. NASDAQ uses the Boston Exchange (now "NASDAQ BX") to pay liquidity takers instead of charge them – a business model catering to guys like Katsuyama's traders at RBC. There is no high-frequency conspiracy behind this; it's just business.

For Lewis, though, the straightforward answer isn't credible if it doesn't implicate high-frequency perfidy:

> "...nothing actually happened by accident: There was a reason for even the oddest events. For instance, one day, investors woke up to discover that they'd bought shares in some company for $30.0001. Why? How was it possible to pay ten-thousandths of a penny for anything? Easy: high-frequency traders had asked for an order type that enabled them to tack digits on the right side of the decimal, so that they might jump the queue in front of people trying to pay $30.00."

Not to be pedantic, but (a) the price Lewis quotes is a hundredth of a penny, not a ten-thousandth, (b) exchanges are legally prohibited from trading in increments of hundredths (or ten-thousandths) of a penny, (c) if it were possible to trade on an exchange in an increment of hundredths of a penny – and it's not possible – then a resting offer to sell at $30.0001 would be behind the superior price of $30.00, and therefore couldn't "jump the queue."[91]

---

[91] Charitably, I think Lewis bungled an attempt to explain "price improvement" in broker internalization facilities in his zeal to accuse high-frequency trading of well, I'm not even sure what his point was in this

Yes, there is a reason for even the oddest events (when they are true). But it's usually pretty mundane.

Really Straining to See Patterns: The Market Reacts to Trades

"I'm straining to see patterns," [Brad] said. "The patterns are being shown to me, but my eyes can't pick them up."

The description of order activity in Bank of America shares is rich in drama but rather cloudy in description. Ironically, the fundamental premise is not particularly dramatic or even insightful: the market reacts to trades. Or, as Lewis writes, "There is an event. Then there is this massive reaction. Then a reaction to that reaction." Katsuyama follows with the question, "If there was no value to reacting, why would anyone react at all?"

For some reason, for Lewis and Katsuyama it is odd, suspicious, even shocking, that the market reacts to a transaction. For what kind of market would possibly react to a change in supply and demand, or new pricing information? Well, pretty much any functioning economic market reacts to supply and demand or new pricing information.

When a trade occurs, it alters the supply of shares available. Returning to high-school economics, a change in supply or demand impacts price. In a properly functioning market, then, one would expect to see a reaction to a trade as participants adjust their prices, supply, and demand to incorporate the new information. And after the first reaction alters the price and supply, you'd expect a smaller, second reaction as market participants adjust again to the recently-

---

example. The corrected example would then be that you purchased shares at the cheaper price of $29.9985, instead of the higher market price of $30.00. The internalizer can then say that you got a better deal than you would have elsewhere, although fifteen cents on one hundred shares isn't exactly a windfall.

altered price and supply. The market reacts, exactly as you would expect it to. This is no more a sign of a high-frequency predator "feeding frenzy" than the sun rising every day.

In a footnote, Lewis admits that the majority of these market reactions – sixty percent – don't appear to be related to a known trade at all! Attempting to salvage another theory torpedoed by the facts, he confidently explains this away, saying these reactions must come "in response to a trade that has occurred in some dark pool." You can't actually see the correlation, he tells us, because the dark pools are not required to report trades in real time, but he's quite sure that it's true. Of course, Lewis says that only 38% of all trades occur in a dark pool.[92] So how would this explain 60% of the reactions?

It's no surprise that Lewis struggles to explain his leap of logic. He doesn't even attempt to explain the "reaction to that reaction," which clearly isn't high-frequency predators reacting to a new trade: none has occurred. Instead, this is simply many market participants re-adjusting their quotes to account for the first changes in supply and pricing dynamics. Say somebody sells 25,000 shares. A big sale could mean the market is starting to drop, so folks with resting bids and offers lower their prices – the first reaction. Now everyone looks around, and some folks decide that maybe somebody over-reacted, and perhaps they can offer a new better price – the reaction to the reaction. It's not a conspiracy, it's not a scam, it's just really basic market economics.

In Lewis' world, though, every press release and market move is yet another sign of high-frequency manipulations. For example, the majority of trades in the stock market are for exactly 100 shares. Lewis told us earlier that these small trades were evidence of the "bait" used by high-frequency traders, and "any decent high-

---

[92] I think Lewis actually means 38% of all trades occur off-exchange, which is consistent with most data on the subject. Of the off-exchange trades, perhaps half occur on dark pools.

frequency trader" would ping a pool with tiny orders like this to search for his "prey." However, since neither Katsuyama nor Lewis worked at a stock exchange, this was purely a guess – they couldn't actually see who was sending these 100-share orders. The opening of IEX, then, would have been a momentous event: it would finally provide the opportunity to see who sends these orders, and possibly gather evidence that the 100-share orders are high-frequency trading bait. Here's what Lewis says happened instead:

> "All [Katsuyama] could see was that a shocking number of the orders being sent by the Wall Street banks to IEX came in small 100-share lots. The HFT guys used 100-share lots as bait on the exchanges, to tease information out of the market while taking as little risk as possible. But these weren't HFT orders; these were from the big banks. At the end of one day, he asked for a count of one bank's orders: 87 percent of them where in these tiny 100-share lots."

So Katsuyama finally has the evidence of the source of the 100-share orders in hand, and...it's a bank, not a high-frequency trader. Shocking indeed. In their first brush with real data, the 100-share-bait theory collapses. How many of their other assumptions about unseen front-running predators would survive the next few weeks? Straining to find any pattern in the data that could salvage these theories, Katsuyama makes himself physically sick.

Lewis, on the other hand, appears quite unconcerned. He doesn't even pause and note that perhaps he had completely missed the boat with this theory, too. Instead, he digs in with two opposing conspiracies about the banks: they are only sending a single 100-share order and intentionally sending the bulk of the order to the other fifty market places, and they are intentionally sending huge numbers of 100-share orders to "sabotage" IEX by creating a lower average trade size. Whatever they do, it's apparently a conspiracy to disadvantage IEX.

"Dark-Pool Arbitrage" Dissected

"Say the market for Procter & Gamble's shares was 80.50 – 80.52, and the quote was stable – the price wasn't about to change. The National Best Bid was $80.50, and the National Best Offer was $80.52, and the stock was just sitting there. A seller of 10,000 Procter & Gamble shares appears on IEX. IEX tried to price the orders that rested on it at the midpoint (the fair price), and so the 10,000 shares were being offered at $80.51. Some high-frequency trader would come into IEX – it was always a high-frequency trader – and chip away at the order: 131 shares here, 189 shares there. But elsewhere in the market, the same HFT was selling the shares – 131 shares here, 189 shares there – at $80.52. On the surface, HFT was performing a useful function, building a bridge between buyer and seller. But the bridge was itself absurd. Why didn't the broker who controlled the buy order simply come to IEX on behalf of his customer and buy, more cheaply, the shares offered?

...[Katsuyama] knew exactly why [these trades] were happening: The Wall Street banks were failing to send their customers' orders to the rest of the marketplace. An investor had given a Wall Street bank an order, say, to buy 10,000 shares of P&G. The bank had sent it to its dark pool with instructions for the order to stay there, aggressively priced, at $80.52..."We're calling this 'dark pool arbitrage,'" said Brad.

Like the other dark pool example involving Chipotle and hedge fund manager Rich Gates (and unlike all the non-dark pool examples), this example is actually possible, if only remotely so. Like Chipotle, it involves dark pools and very bad choices. Also like Chipotle, Lewis has to admit that everyone involved gets exactly what they asked for.

In fact, in the middle of the example Lewis explains that, if they were to employ this strategy, high-frequency traders would be "performing a useful function." The seller in the dark pool completed his trade at the price he wanted. The buyer also completed his trade at the price desired. Neither party would have been able to find the other because they both chose to hide their orders in dark pools, where, by definition, the other party can't find them. From that perspective, Lewis is quite right that "building a bridge between buyer and seller" was "performing a useful function."[93]

Unfortunately, once Lewis attempts to explain why these trades occur he yet again misses the mark.

The only actual observations – if the example isn't completely hypothetical – were probably that there were trades of 131 shares and 189 shares in IEX at $80.51, and there were trades in the same quantities at $80.52 on other markets.[94] That's pretty much the extent of the facts.

It's all Lewis' speculation after that point, and pretty far-fetched at that: he imagines a broker, who has a customer order; who decides to place it as a *resting* bid instead of the usual immediately executable market order; only he doesn't match the current price of resting bids, but instead tries to buy at the higher price of the *current resting offers;* although such an order would normally match immediately and execute at that price, the broker prevents this by hiding his customer's order in a *second dark pool;* lastly, the order happens to have the *exact same number of shares* as the order in IEX. Each of these conditions are required to make Lewis' explanation

---

[93] Curiously, he simultaneously describes this as "predation" and a way to "exploit investors." The rhetorical schizophrenia continues as, after thrice declaring that the price was absolutely stable in his example, he explains that this is an example of high-frequency traders detecting *price movements* "to exploit" "ordinary investors' ignorance."

[94] At the risk of repeating myself, there is no way to know who has participated in a trade on another market, nor the quantities of shares that they sought with their orders, nor the type of order they submitted. This is doubly or triply true if the other market is a dark pool. Thus, everything Lewis says about any buy order at $80.52 is a wild guess.

possible – it falls apart otherwise – and each of them requires extremely unusual choices, to say the least.

Despite all these creative twists and turns, Lewis still never explains why the trades occur in such strange quantities. No professional trades in odd quantities like 131 or 189 shares unless they have to, since the "odd lots" that don't round to one hundred have historically been more expensive to process in the "back-office" after the trade is made. These strange quantities, however, are the key to really understanding what's going on.

As any experienced trader will tell you, sometimes odd lots are necessary when you need to precisely offset or hedge your risk in something else. For example, P&G is a large component of the Dow Jones Industrials stock index. If you sold 3,000 shares of the Dow index fund, you might hedge that sale by purchasing the number of shares of P&G that trade represents – about 190 shares. Or if you sold 2,000 shares of the Dow index fund, you might hedge that sale by purchasing the number of shares of P&G that trade represents – about 130 shares. (The ratios change over time, and vary slightly based on the precise model used.)

So imagine this: some trader sells 3,000 shares of DIA, an exchange-traded index fund that represents the Dow Jones index. He wants to immediately hedge his risk in P&G and looks to buy the equivalent number of shares. He could buy those shares at the displayed offer in the public markets of $80.52. But if a dark pool like IEX had shares available at $80.51, he'd save a penny. So why not try? If IEX didn't have the shares, his order would just miss, he would just go to the public markets and try again to complete the hedge. A third-party observer would see this as a string of trades of 189 shares at $80.51 and $80.52 – which is exactly what we see in this anecdote.

It's pretty straightforward. No gymnastics necessary. No mythical broker placing a resting bid at the offer price into a dark pool. Anyone who has ever had to offset the risk of a position would immediately recognize these odd lot quantities for what they were – hedging trades. In fairness, perhaps Katsuyama only handled basic customer orders, and had limited interaction with more complicated hedging trades.

Despite this unfamiliarity with the business, or any other credible explanation for these two trades, Katsuyama's "Puzzle Masters" somehow go on to estimate that "dark pool arbitrage" – the strategy just dissected as a good way to lose money – makes more than a billion dollars a year. Let's ignore, for now, the fact that this estimate approaches the consensus estimates for *total profits* for all high-frequency trading firms.[95] Let's also ignore the fact that the strategy itself seems rather unprofitable. Let's just consider how they could have arrived at this estimate.

How did the "Puzzle Masters" estimate "dark pool arbitrage" when there's not even any market data for dark pools? How, when dark pool trades aren't necessarily published in real time? When you can't know who made what trade or why? It's not clear on what data they based this model – or any of their models of their purported high-frequency predation strategies – but we can be fairly certain that their models were never tested by the real world.

Wall Street is littered with the carcasses of trading models that seemed hugely profitable in Excel, but don't actually work in the real world. For example, the price of Sony shares traded in Tokyo differs from the price of Sony shares traded on the NYSE – here's millions of dollars in arbitrage profit! Try to trade it. They actually aren't the same shares. Trying to convert or exchange them is an expensive, cumbersome process. One other thing: the Tokyo Stock Exchange and the NYSE aren't open at the same time, so you couldn't run an arbitrage strategy even if you solved the logistical problems.

---

[95] Incidentally, based on the volume of shares traded in dark pools in 2013 and the per-share profits Lewis describes, this strategy would tally $1 billion only if it accounted for more than 50% of all dark pool trades. This is, of course, absurd.

Such models are always constructed using "perfect" market data, which as we know doesn't actually exist. In fact, inaccuracies in your market data (i.e. "bugs" or "glitches" in your data source) are exactly what would look like the most profitable opportunities. In a market as intensely competitive as the U.S. equity markets, these opportunities are as rare as unicorns. Try to trade on them, and you'll see that either you missed some key assumption – like Tokyo is asleep when New York is awake – or that your market data is erroneous. Even error-free data can be misleading. You may think that every fleeting change in price is an opportunity to profit, but instead these opportunities turn out to be utterly impossible to capture in the real world – by the time your order is ready to send, the real market already changed.

It's not even a matter of speed. If a market-maker simultaneously adjusts his bids and offers on multiple markets, your market data shows a fleeting arbitrage opportunity as you receive data from one market before another. In reality, the prices are already updated everywhere, your data just doesn't show it. You might think this is an arbitrage opportunity, but in fact none exists.

The only way to really find out what works, and what doesn't, is to try it.

This is one reason why it's so maddening that Lewis never sat down with any real high-frequency traders to test his theories. They would have regaled him with stories of strategies that made a million dollars on paper but lost thousands of dollars a day in the real markets. I myself have an embarrassing amount of such stories. Without that context, though, the errors and impossibilities of *Flash Boys* aren't terribly surprising.[96] Everyone looks at the markets and imagines some unseen pattern or strategy worth millions, or even billions. It's the second national pastime, played out on CNBC instead

---

[96] With now typical inconsistency, in Chapter 8, Lewis roundly mocks an "expert witness" at the trial of Sergey Aleynikov for his ignorance: he "still had never actually done any high-frequency trading himself."

of ESPN. Just like ESPN, there are a lot of armchair quarterbacks whose theories sound good in the living room, but would fall apart completely in the real world.

Throwing Down the Gauntlet: The Results of the IEX Experiment

In Chapter 6, Lewis presented IEX as a sort of experiment. By welcoming high-frequency traders, it provided a possible answer to the question of whether or not high-frequency trading firms could provide value when neither speed nor complexity was involved. He wonders whether high-frequency traders would come to IEX, "if orders couldn't be exploited on this new exchange."

As it turns out, not many of his hedge fund investors traded on IEX on day one. However, apparently a high-frequency market-maker did. As Katsuyama related in an interview, "[they] said 'We'll be there on day one.' And they were there."[97] They were, in fact, the only broker mentioned by name in the press on the day after IEX started trading.[98]

Incidentally, this firm is the same one that Lewis pilloried earlier for not losing money often enough. Despite Lewis' claim that their performance was "possible only if you have a huge informational advantage," they apparently had no qualms about diving into a market explicitly designed to eliminate any informational advantages.

Katsuyama later called them "a good contributor of value to our market," and noted that this single firm accounted for a remarkable

---

[97] See "Katsuyama, Narang, Lewis Debate Speed Trading," Bloomberg TV, April 2, 2014.

[98] See "New U.S. trading platform, IEX, aims to disrupt market structure," John McCrank, Reuters, October 28, 2013.

7.5% of IEX's volume.[99] They consistently make markets on IEX, providing liquidity for IEX's investors to access. And they aren't the only one. By July of 2014, high-frequency traders accounted for almost twenty percent of all trading on IEX.[100]

Thus, there is an unequivocal answer to the IEX experiment Lewis set up: high-frequency trading (a) does not require any sort of informational advantage, and (b) can provide significant value to markets. As one IEX investor later reflected, "there are HFT strategies that are beneficial to the market and create true liquidity."[101]

As a side-note, in his discussion of "dark pool arbitrage," Lewis writes, "In the first two months of its existence, IEX had seen no activity from high-frequency traders except [predatory trading]." Obviously, it's hard to reconcile what Lewis says about the first few months of IEX's existence with what IEX's CEO himself says. To put it bluntly, only one of them could be right.

Lewis set up an experiment that he thought would prove that high-frequency trading used unfair advantages and ripped everyone off. That's not what happened. He saw the results. It's a shame he couldn't admit that he was wrong.[102]

---

[99] *Ibid.* See also "IEX Welcomes High-Speed Traders, as Long as They Behave," Sam Mamudi, Bloomberg, March 31, 2014.

[100] See "'Flash Boys' and the Speed of Lies," Brad Katsuyama, Bloomberg View, August 3, 2014. See also "Debate Over High-Frequency Trading on IEX Muddied by Trade Counting," Bradley Hope, The Wall Street Journal, August 11, 2014.

[101] See "IEX Welcomes High-Speed Traders, as Long as They Behave," Sam Mamudi, Bloomberg, March 31, 2014.

[102] After hearing Katsuyama relate the above facts on national television, Lewis finally allowed, "It's different from one high-frequency firm to another. Obviously."

Who Are the Good Brokers?

> *"IEX follows a price-priority model first, then by displayed order second. Then comes broker priority, which means a broker will always trade with itself first, which Katsuyama described as "free internalization." He explained that brokers do not pay IEX to trade should an order be matched against another order from that same broker. This, he added, offers brokers incentive to trade in IEX."*[103]

How many "good brokers" are there? Apparently only ten, and, per Lewis, Goldman Sachs is the most important.

Most readers were more than a bit surprised to see that the white knight who saves the day in *Flash Boys* is Goldman Sachs. Even if it only saves the day for fifty-one minutes on December 19, 2013.

Lewis does a decent job of analyzing the big reason behind this: Goldman isn't that good at high-frequency trading. It simply doesn't attract the same talent pool as small, agile firms where flip-flops are the norm. The anemic per-trade profit margins don't work well in a firm like Goldman, where it's more expensive to handle back office operations (and investors expect very high profit margins). Their technology is burdened by hundreds of legacy requirements.

But it's also worth noting that Goldman had to get out of high-frequency trading anyway. The Volcker Rule, a product of the Financial Crisis, prohibits banks like Goldman from doing any proprietary trading in the future. They have until July 2015 to wind everything down. So if Goldman didn't shutter their high-frequency trading now, it would have happened sometime in the next sixteen months.

Goldman could have issued a press release saying, "We're quitting high-frequency trading since we have to, and we're not very

---

[103] See "The Buyside Takes Control," John D'Antona, Jr., Traders Magazine, October 2013.

good at it, anyway." Instead, they shrewdly spun their retreat and hooked Lewis into writing one of the first positive pieces on Goldman Sachs since 2007.

Needless to say, I don't really buy Lewis' rationalization that Goldman is supporting IEX because it thinks that doing so will decrease the risk of a market "calamity" that could jeopardize the $7 billion in annual profits in their equity business. I'm sure that if Goldman really believed that $7 billion were at stake, they'd do more than send their order flow to a different dark pool for a fraction of one day in December.

Incidentally, seven billion dollars is five to seven times the profits of the entire high-frequency trading industry. Thus, even if Goldman were one of the most profitable high-frequency trading firms, it would merely add a drop in the bucket at bonus time. This belies the real risk-reward calculation for Goldman: why deal with the firestorm around high-frequency trading when it's less than a rounding error in your profits?

There's one other reason for Goldman to like IEX. With IEX, banks get a free, private dark pool. Katsuyama calls it "free internalization" in the quote above. A cynic would call it "washing their hands." The idea is simple: banks can still trade against their customer orders, but instead of doing it inside their own dark pool – which, understandably, sounds fairly sketchy – they can do it on IEX. With "free internalization," the banks still get the first look at their customer's orders on IEX, even if other brokers were ahead of them in the queue. The banks can still internalize the orders, but now it looks external. Best of all, it's free, and they can bask in the good press coverage. The catch is that if the bank chooses not to trade against their customer order, they can't sell it off to the next guy in the payment-for-order-flow cascade – instead, everyone else (in the dark pool at least) has a shot at filling the order.

The banks win, IEX wins, and other traders on IEX win. The public markets, not so much. On the other hand, it's far better than the status quo of internalization and banks trading in their own dark pools.[104]

The Market is Rigged. Let's Sue It.

"The stock market at bottom was rigged. The icon of global capitalism was a fraud. How would enterprising politicians and plaintiff's lawyers and state attorneys general respond to that news?"

It's hard not to imagine Lewis smirking as he wrote these lines. It took less than three weeks for an "enterprising" plaintiff's lawyer to file a class action lawsuit, largely quoting from *Flash Boys*. Politicians of all stripes announced new investigations into high-frequency trading.

Lewis obviously expected to set off a firestorm with his scurrilous polemic (as he proudly told one interviewer, "I kicked Wall Street in the balls"). I suppose he's entitled to do so, but if one is going to yell "Fire!" in a crowded theater, one has a responsibility to make sure that one is right. Lewis clearly abdicated that responsibility.

Every intelligent market observer – from journalists to regulators – has roundly rejected the statement that the markets are

---

[104] Ironically, "free internalization" also eliminates one of the barriers to front-running: normally, any would-be front-runner wouldn't be able to step in front of a customer's order because other resting orders in the market already have priority. With "free internalization" they could, in theory, place their order a microsecond ahead of an intentionally delayed customer order and jump to the head of the queue to trade against their customer. This isn't possible on the public price-time priority stock exchanges.

rigged. Lewis' hero, Ronan Ryan, is himself quite clear: "I don't think the markets are rigged."[105]

What a waste of energy. Nuisance lawsuits aside, does it really make sense for the FBI and the Department of Justice to open new investigations on the turf already patrolled by at least three overlapping regulators? It only makes sense because a best-selling author has cried wolf.

As Lewis surveys the wreckage of his first two hundred pages, it seems that even he senses his own recklessness. He almost sounds apologetic as he admits, "It's even healthy and good when some clever high-frequency trader divines a necessary statistical relationship between the share prices of Chevron and Exxon, and responds when it gets out of whack." In fact, he then constructs a litany of examples of arbitrage, each of which he deems "healthy and good." In the end, the only thing that remains neither healthy nor good to him is "when public stock exchanges introduced order types and speed advantages that high-frequency traders could use to exploit everyone else."

"The market is rigged" boils down to this? Does it really make sense for the FBI to drop their criminal investigations to focus on a Hide-Not-Slide order – particularly when Lewis' explanations of the order and its purported evil uses are dead wrong? Does it really make sense for the Department of Justice to opine on the speed of exchange matching engines – when Lewis' examples of "slow market arbitrage" are fatally flawed, and even his protagonist decries that a millisecond doesn't matter to investors?

No, the market is not rigged. Trading costs for investors have plummeted in the past fifteen years. The quantity of shares available at the best bid or offer has doubled. The monopolies of yesteryear – each a single point-of-failure – have been replaced by a diverse community of markets and liquidity providers. It's not perfect.

---

[105] See "IEX not anti-HFT, says founder," John Bakie, The TRADE, April 9, 2014.

Problems like the opacity of dark pools and internalizers, perverse incentives of payment for order flow, and fragmentation from too many market centers are real. But these issues, which the industry and SEC have been working on since 2010, shouldn't obscure the basic fact that the markets work. They work tremendously well, and they work to the benefit of the general public.

CHAPTER 8:

MY DINNER WITH SERGEY

I won't spend much time on Lewis' expense-account dinner party, except to say that his "experts" were either not so expert, or just not understood by Lewis.

For example, I'm not sure where Lewis gets the idea that deleting one's bash history is a "common practice." In Chapter 5 we already saw that it was unnecessary on two counts: (a) protecting his password from the system administrators – the only people who can view his bash history, and the only people who can already read any file he has – is pointless, and (b) even rookies know that you're not supposed to use a password on the command line, anyway. The only reason somebody "needs" to delete their command history is that they don't want anyone to know what they are doing. Lewis sums up the discussion with what he calls the "obvious" question: "If deleting the bash history was so clever and devious, why had Goldman ever found out he'd taken anything?" The technical answer is that when you delete your bash history, you replace the entire log of everything you have done on your computer with a single entry which says that you deleted your bash history. Effectively, you replace the security video tapes for the last six hours with a single thirty-second clip of you erasing all the security footage. Any reasonable system administrator would find this highly suspicious, and would review other activity logs to piece together what happened.

Fundamentally, though, the idea underpinning this question is rather naive: you can't call Aleynikov clever or devious, because he got caught. I'm not a lawyer, but I don't think this is a good argument for the defense to make. By this logic, no criminal should be called devious, since they got caught.

Lastly, there is the question of why Sergey did not take Goldman's "secret sauce" strategies. Lewis answered the question two pages prior, but apparently didn't catch it: "Goldman's code was of no use whatsoever in the system [Malyshev had] hired Serge to build...it had been designed for a firm that was trading with its own customers, and Teza, Malyshev's firm, didn't have customers." The trading strategies might have been the secret sauce, but for a different recipe. For Goldman, customers were a key ingredient. Thus, the only thing of common value between the two firm's trading systems would have been modifications to the operating system and network processing code.

I don't know what was contained in the 500,000 lines of source code that Aleynikov took. I do know that most trading systems use proprietary code for strategies, but rely on open source operating systems and network processing code. This open source software is often modified for the particular network requirements of trading. And these modifications are quite valuable – they make *every single order* faster or slower, depending on how clever one is. I wish somebody had asked hard questions.

EPILOGUE

There's not too much to say about Lewis' bike ride with the Women's Adventure Club. Everything about Spread applies to microwave towers: speed is important and some people will pay for it.

After running pell-mell through the rest of the book, the calm and attention to detail in this section are striking. I wish Lewis had taken the time to get the details right in the prior two hundred pages.

Lewis has since allowed, "It's impossible to write 100,000 words, and not make mistakes," but he claims that no subsequent revisions "will have any effect on the truth of the overall story, at all."[106]

I agree with (and sympathize with) the first part. I'm sure there are mistakes in my work, too. But it was rather bold to claim that no future revisions will affect the main argument of the book, just eleven days after it hit the shelves. Such a claim makes one wonder how Lewis plans to tackle any mistakes that threaten his narrative: will he ignore them? Will he re-arrange the "facts" of his trading anecdotes to make them fit his conclusion?

It will be good for him to correct the statistics that he flubbed: profitability, market volatility, investor confidence, and trends in

---

[106] See "Michael Lewis hits back: 'There's been a lot of people mouthing off without actually thinking about the book,'" Andrew Leonard, Salon, April 11, 2014.

trading costs, for example. On the face of it, the corrected numbers would undermine his argument, but perhaps he can make it work. As for the personal anecdotes – upon which the core of his "front-running" thesis rests – I don't think they can be salvaged. One can't just say, "I remembered it wrong the first time, let me try again." Regardless, the anecdotes, like the trading examples, rest on a false understanding of how the markets work. Sadly, I don't think Lewis wants to fix those falsehoods.

For my part, I've tried my best to fix Lewis' errors. I recognize that I will be vilified in certain quarters for doing so. More than once, I've asked myself why I should bother sticking my neck out, particularly for an industry in which I no longer work. The answer I keep coming back to is this: I believe that the changes in our capital markets in the last decade – computerization, competition, broader and fairer access than ever before – have resulted in tremendous benefits for every investor in the stock market. Never before in history have we seen such a rapid reduction in trading costs, which flows through to every investor. Rolling back these changes would have a real and negative impact on our financial system, our retirement accounts, and our wallets. If this book can replace the angry unsubstantiated allegations of *Flash Boys* with calm, rational policy discussion, then it was worth it.

SUMMING IT UP

"Anything that could be said about [financial actions] could be believed."

- Michael Lewis, Flash Boys

Michael Lewis believes the stock market is rigged.

It is rigged, he says, by a conspiracy of high-frequency traders, the stock exchanges, the regulators, retail brokers, and the banks. Over half of all stock market activity, he claims, consists of high-frequency traders front-running investors.

Lewis' allegations of an omnipresent front-running scheme rest almost entirely upon three anecdotes and three hypothetical examples. The anecdotes consist of some bank or hedge fund trader executing a large trade, and the market reacting to the change in supply/demand by changing price. While there is a simple economic explanation for this – the law of supply and demand – which Lewis acknowledges in selected other contexts, for these anecdotes he unequivocally blames the market's reaction on a conspiratorial front-running scheme.

Remarkably, he makes no attempt to supply evidence that anyone actually traded ahead of or against these orders, or even that any other trades occurred at the time – both prerequisites for any front-running scheme. His entire theory is based solely upon the fact that the market showed a new price after a large trade, and nothing else. In an industry awash in data, where millions of trades are analyzed every day, Lewis offers the lame excuse that he can't find any data to prove his case because the data doesn't exist. This is simply not credible.

Lewis' hypothetical examples of front-running also don't work. Misunderstanding basic principles built-in to today's markets, such as trade-through protection, price-time priority, and protection of order information, he conjures up scenarios that are impossible. The tricks of thirty years ago simply aren't possible in today's computerized markets, which automatically enforce these rules. Brokers can no longer stick a customer with an off-market price. All trades, broker or customer, must occur only at the prices set by the entire national market. Customer order information is only revealed if the customer chooses to do so. Lewis never even attempts to explain how a would-be front-runner guesses the quantity and price of a customer's order, because he has no plausible explanation. Without order information and the ability to stick a customer with an off-market price, these alleged scams are not possible.

Even if they weren't based on impossible assumptions, the predatory scams Lewis alleges wouldn't eke out the tenths of a cent of profit that he alleges. Instead, they would be guaranteed to consistently lose many times more money. In short, what Lewis alleges is impossible, and if it weren't, only a fool would attempt it.

The gaping holes in *Flash Boys'* arguments are painfully obvious to anyone who has ever traded electronically. By avoiding the people who know the topic best – let alone anyone working at a high-frequency trading firm or a stock exchange – Lewis ran a real risk of missing the mark completely. And he did. He also deprived himself of the other side of the story.

The other side of the story is that the computerization of the markets wrought by high-frequency traders – specifically market-makers – has dramatically reduced transaction costs for all investors. Even Lewis admits that the cost of buying and selling shares is *six times lower* in the era of electronic trading. This is an extraordinary result, and these benefits flow directly to the investor. The fat cats who used to pocket this money – a cadre of specialists and big bank equity traders – have been replaced by a diverse multitude of firms constantly competing to offer better prices. Some of the old Wall Street swagger is gone, and so is part of the risk.

It's hardly a footnote now, but the U.S. stock market was pretty much the only part of the financial system that kept functioning throughout the Financial Crisis of 2007-2008. Like the housing market, stock valuations plummeted, but unlike the housing market one could buy or sell at any time, at a market-determined price. We may not have liked the prices, but we never lost the ability to manage our investments. And managing those investments has never been cheaper or more efficient than it is today.

Few, if any, economists would say that the stock market is the highest priority in financial reform today. It's not perfect, but it is more efficient and better regulated than the markets for bonds, currencies, swaps, gold, mortgage-backed securities (remember those from the Financial Crisis?), silver – the list goes on and on. That said, it can be made better.

The one credible example in the book – a hedge fund that gets the price they asked for, but not the price they wanted in a dark pool – raises legitimate questions about dark pools, and rightly so. These private markets (including Katsuyama's dark pool, IEX) play by a different set of rules than the public markets, and it's reasonable to ask whether that is healthy for our financial system. It's reasonable to probe the payment for order flow system, and ask whether it really benefits retail customers. It's a shame that these real issues get buried under Lewis' bombastic polemics on high-frequency trading.

Is all high-frequency trading beneficial to the markets? No. To suggest otherwise would be naive – there have always been bad actors on Wall Street and there always will be. However, it's even more naive to suggest that everyone using a computer – pretty much any professional in the market – is part of a vast conspiracy of front-running.

No, the market isn't rigged. It's not perfect, but it's in better shape than it ever has been. Yet there's still plenty of work to be done.

ABOUT THE AUTHOR

PETER KOVAC served as the Chief Operating Officer of EWT, one of the largest electronic market-making firms in the U.S., from 2004 to 2011, managing regulatory compliance, risk management, finance, trading operations, and portions of the technology teams. During his tenure, EWT traded hundreds of millions of shares daily, and, together with its affiliates traded in over 50 markets worldwide. He has been a frequent commenter to the S.E.C. on regulatory and policy issues. Prior to his role at EWT, Mr. Kovac worked in Silicon Valley as a programmer and software architect. He graduated from Princeton University with a degree in Electrical Engineering and a certificate in Public Policy from the Woodrow Wilson School of Public and International Affairs.